real
L♥VE

HOW TO AVOID ROMANTIC CHAOS
AND FIND THE PATH TO LASTING LOVE

real
andy thompson
L♥VE

TATE PUBLISHING
AND ENTERPRISES, LLC

Published by Tate Publishing & Enterprises, LLC
127 E. Trade Center Terrace | Mustang, Oklahoma 73064 USA
1.888.361.9473 | www.tatepublishing.com

Tate Publishing is committed to excellence in the publishing industry. The company reflects the philosophy established by the founders, based on Psalm 68:11,
"The Lord gave the word and great was the company of those who published it."

Book design copyright © 2013 by Tate Publishing, LLC. All rights reserved.
Cover design by Samson Lim
Interior design by Mary Jean Archival

Published in the United States of America

ISBN: 978-1-61862-802-2
1. Religion / Christian Life / Love & Marriag
2. Family & Relationships / Love & Romance
13.02.12

To my Father, who talked to me when I was a boy and planted the seeds of wisdom within me. He had already given me life, and determined to sustain it, he gave me the greatest gift of all. He taught me to think, and to follow Wisdom above all.

Introduction

No matter who you are, where you come from, or what your nationality is, love is a concept that we all understand, and is something that we all need. Unfortunately, because of our differences, we can all have different definitions of what love is, how to express love, and how we receive it. That difference, very often, is the very thing that causes so many relationships to fail.

It is not that we are bad people, have evil in our intentions, or are determined to hurt one another. Yet, all of us have at some point been hurt by love. As a matter of fact, I would be willing to bet that some of the most painful experiences of your life have occurred at the hands of someone you loved or someone you thought loved you.

But that is not what we want. We don't go through the painful process of having and raising children, only for them to come to a place where they are not sure of our love. That disconnect is often a result, not of intention, but of expression.

We do not meet someone, court them, pull up the courage to tell them that we love them and marry them, just so that we can hurt them, wound them, betray them, and then leave them in less than five years. However, that is what the statistics say we are doing. But I know that is not our intention.

We want to love forever; we want love to last.

It is a binding quality, something every person in the world shares. We all want eternal love. Every mother, regardless of race or culture, will fight for her child, and will become distraught if you were to take her child away from her. She had the child to love it forever, not for two years, but forever.

Every person on the planet takes that plunge with eternity in mind when they meet that special someone, that life partner, the one they desire to share life, breath, sex, and living space with. We all want love to last; we want Real Love.

The challenge is that lasting love is not something you stumble into; it is intentional. Anyone who can say that they love their spouse more today that yesterday, and they mean it, has done some work. We want to believe that love just happens, that it is bound to search for us, that providence, God even, will just bring us love if we just sit back and wait for it.

Unfortunately, in the 21st century, we understand that this is not the case. And if you do a study of human history, you will find that this has almost never been the case, especially considering the fact that marriage for love is a fairly recent phenomenon. You could argue that Adam and Eve had an arranged marriage. God didn't create Eve, and then have Adam ask her out for coffee, date her for ten months, then start to look for a ring, think maybe they should live together first... you get the picture.

I suppose that Adam and Eve were an extreme case. What other options did they have? But most of human history has followed this line of reasoning in the path to marriage. In most cultures, a wife was something that a man acquired.

Now I know that women have taken extreme offense to this idea: the very thought that they were treated as cattle, connected to family fortunes, and were used to forge alliances with no say in the matter. And I agree, although I would be willing to bet that there may be some women out there who would love it if their parents found them a great guy. They would love to have a "matchmaker," like in *Fiddler on the Roof*. But I digress...

There was a time in human history when love followed duty; it was function over feeling. You were promised to someone and met this person, knew him or her for a very short time, and then were married, believing that you would come to love your new spouse. I know that very often the love never came; we saw the inequality of the system and realized that women were being mistreated, and even men were often disappointed with this system.

So we decided to become enlightened, to change our perspective and to "Marry for love." It is a wonderful idea, and I am glad that I got to marry the person that I wanted, not some person that my dad picked for me because he wanted to ally his country/company to some guy he met once. I was the one who choose the hips, not my mother, who thought this one had good bone structure or that one had the right kind of hair. No, I got to choose. You get to choose. We get to choose.

And there is power in that choice and freedom in that ability to make that decision. But there has been a price for that freedom. The price is fifty percent of marriages end in divorce; close to 70% of the children grow up without the father in the home, widespread sexually transmitted diseases, and pain, pain that afflicts the soul.

Where did we go wrong?

I believe in the power that we have to choose. I don't want to go back to the old system, but at the same time, for a marriage to work, for love to last, there needs to be a balance. We need to marry for love and duty, for feelings and function. There need to be times when Feelings get behind the wheel, but after a few miles, Feelings must pull over and let Function drive for a bit. If we can strike the right balance of love and duty, feelings and function, then we can stem the tide of marital disunity and family dysfunction. We can have what God intended when He created marriage, when He brought Eve to Adam, and we will actually be able to love someone to death.

Chapter 1

The Goal—Marriage

W hen most of us think about dating, we think about finding someone, how to meet someone and making the connection. And that is important, the search. But it is difficult to search when you don't know what you are looking for. And that is a part of the challenge of dating. People date for different reasons because they have different goals. So before we talk about searching, we first have to agree on what the goal of dating is.

That is what has made dating so difficult to explain and define. We can't seem to agree on what the goal of dating should be. People date for fun; people date for sex; people date so that they won't be alone. But the real goal of dating should be marriage. There is nothing worse than spending years with someone, in an exclusive relationship, which ends without permanent connection.

That can be particularly devastating for a woman. You don't want to give a man four years of your youth, only for him to leave you. And there are many women I have counseled who were in their thirties and alone because they "dated" some guy for five years when they were in their twenties. But that is not dating;

that is wasting time. A Real-Love dating relationship shouldn't last longer than eighteen months and should end in Holy Matrimony.

Once we agree that marriage is the goal, we then have to agree on what marriage is. And there is another challenge. One of the reasons marriage is so difficult to do is that we have so many definitions of it. We think that we can define it the way that we want to; we have seen so many different types of marriages that we think that there are different types of marriage. Many of us have never seen a good marriage, so we don't even know what to look for or how to define a good one.

And since one of the core foundations of marriage is agreement, it makes marriage difficult to do. We can't agree, and there isn't a common voice or one definition that we can gravitate to that can help us to come together. So if we have a common definition of marriage, then we will have a clearer path to follow when it comes to dating.

So let's talk about marriage for a bit.

Marriage – The Picture

Marriage is supposed to be the ultimate picture of love. It is love combined with eternal commitment. Marriage is supposed to stand the test of time, and is a common thread in human culture. We all want love that lasts, and I have never heard of a culture in which an eternal commitment between a man and a woman was not a part of the culture. That does not mean that it does not exist, but if there is such a culture, it is extremely rare. Humans believe in marriage.

And when we were growing up and thought of marriage, we did not think of it as a temporary thing or as something that would last for five years and end in anger and pain. When we think of eternal love, we think of someone to grow old with, someone to have children with, and someone to share life with.

And a good marriage is a wonderful thing; it is the vehicle that creates family; family is the foundation to a stable humanity. So when we talk about marriage and start to use dating to find Real Love, that person to marry, we have to be aware of the romantic side, but also the functional side of the marriage relationship.

So let's define it; let's break it down to its most basic elements. There are so many pieces to a good marriage.

1) Love and Friendship

It is one thing to love someone, but it's something else altogether different to *like* that person. Good marriages have both; the couple loves and likes each other. They have a romantic relationship, but they are also really good friends.

When we recognize that the friendship is as important as the sexual love component, we are on our way to a healthy relationship. I am not saying that a healthy sexual relationship is not important. Good sex is always a part of the foundation of any good marriage. But good sex comes as a result of emotional intimacy, especially consistent sex with the same person.

I suppose to some people's way of thinking, the one-night stand can have its own level of excitement, surrounded by danger. But it is really not something that should be anyone's goal, a life full of recreational, empty sexual encounters. Not only can they affect you physically, but also they can damage you emotionally. The goal is good consistent sex with one person, your mate. And for that sex to stay good, there has to be emotional intimacy and connection. The two go hand in hand.

It is difficult to have good sex with your wife if you are not friends with her, especially after some years have gone by. It does not matter how good she looks; if you do not like her, then eventually you will not want to be intimate with her. And that applies even more to women. If you do not like who your husband is, you are not going to want to have sex with him. And the more you reject him or show little physical interest in him, the more he will not like you. Consequently, a vicious cycle is created.

So when you are dating, you need to be determined to develop the friendship first. So many people date to find sexual compatibility, but emotional compatibility trumps sexual connection. Dating should develop friendship so that the love is not love alone. Because as important as "love" is, liking the person is even more important. It is easier to do when it is *love* and *like* for life.

2) Duty

There was a time when marriage was just about duty. I am glad that we have moved away from that. We have the ability to choose now; our marriages are not arranged. There was a time when the duty came first, and you hoped for love to follow.

Now we have become more enlightened, we understand how important love and friendship is. But let's not throw the baby out with the bath water. Duty is an important part of a good marriage. I have a responsibility so that even when I may not feel like doing right, I answer the call of duty.

There are some responsibilities that go beyond how you feel at that moment. Just because you may be upset, does not give you an excuse to act any way that you want. Marriage is a job; it is a role that you play. You don't go to work only when you feel like it. If you did, you would not have that job for very long.

In the same way, I have a responsibility to talk to my wife, to listen to her. She has a responsibility to communicate with me, to connect with me. It goes beyond how we feel at that moment. Somewhere in our society's enlightenment, we have lost the foundation of good commitment. A marriage can't be good if it is unpredictable and inconsistent.

So when you are dating someone, you are looking for someone who shows consistency and faithfulness. If they seem to only do what they want to do, or like to do, then that is a sign to you of how they will be in a marriage. If you see immaturity or a lack of discipline, these traits are going to be a serious factor in a marriage relationship.

3) Submitted Agreement

I know the word *submission* can be a scary word. And when we think of submission, we mostly think of it applying to women. But for a marriage to work, the real answer is *submitted agreement*. Submission is not enough. And submission only applies when you do not agree.

Now there will be times when you do not agree in marriage. During those times, you have several options as to how you will proceed to make your relationship work. You can:

A) Fight and continue to disagree—this may sound crazy, but it is exactly where most couples land. They disagree and can never quite find the solution to their disagreement, which turns into a perpetual fight.

B) Find a third party who can help to mediate the dispute. This can be effective at times. Sometimes you disagree because one of you is wrong, and there isn't anyone to tell that person they are wrong. Or, you may both be wrong and right at the same time. There can be so many different scenarios. To find someone you both trust, someone who can be impartial, and someone you both respect, can go a along way to dissolving a dispute.

It is better to head off disputes as quickly as possible. So if you can, meet with a counselor, minister, or even an older family member; find someone who knows something about marriage and what it takes to work, someone who can really assist you in your determination to keep your relationship healthy.

OR

C) Clearly define roles, based on strengths and weaknesses. This is the best solution. Obviously, you do not want a fight to go on forever, and it can be difficult to constantly be dependent on a third party to settle disputes. If you can decide who has strength or the superior knowledge in different areas, and then agree to submit to one another in those areas, that can be extremely valuable in times of disagreement.

For example, if one of you is better with money than the other, then that person ought to have a bit more "say," so to speak, and in times of disagreement, there should be some submitted agreement. In my marriage, my wife is great with money, great with the kids and their education and great with keeping track of everyone's health needs, so in those areas, we all submit. We have agreed to submit. Even though I am the husband, if we have a disagreement about one of those areas, I have agreed to submit.

We don't fight about issues forever, and we don't need someone else to tell us what to do. We find solutions between ourselves. When you have a couple, and both people are very strong, this kind of role-defining agreement is often an excellent solution, and it can help you to avoid endless, needless bickering and arguments.

So when you are dating someone, you are looking for someone who has strengths where you have weaknesses, and someone who has the humility to admit that they are not perfect and will be looking to rely on your expertise in the areas in which you have expertise. Once again, the goal of marriage helps to define what we are looking for in our dating experience.

4) Faithful Consistency

Marriage is a test of one's ability to be consistent and faithful in spite of the circumstances. That is what marriage is—trust in the faithfulness of another's commitment. When I got married, I entered into a binding contract, an agreement to be faithful to one person.

Now I know that there are people who "swing" or have "open marriages," but that is not what marriage is about. Infidelity can be such a devastating force in a good marriage. In a Real Love relationship, you should not need more than one sexual partner. You ought to be able to find satisfaction in one person. That is a part of what makes your relationship so special and unique.

But faithfulness goes beyond just my physical relationship. I have to be Faithful to:

- Communicate consistently
- Be accountable when it comes to whereabouts
- Be consistent to the traditions that we have instituted—things like vacations and date nights, etc.

Marriage is not a sprint; it is a marathon. You run a marathon differently than a sprint. In a marathon, you pace yourself; you realize that you are not going to be in the same place in mile three that you will be in mile fifteen. If you are impatient about getting to mile fifteen, then you will never get there.

In the same way, I have to be patient, to allow my relationship to develop properly over time. If you are in too much of a hurry, you can damage the relationship, and it may affect your ability to finish your race. You are not going to be at year three where you are going to be at year fifteen. Don't get too upset if you do not totally understand each other at year four; if you keep on running, by year seventeen, you will be finishing each other's sentences.

But many couples never get there. Marriage is just something that they are trying. Most divorces happen within the first five years. Some of that is due to impatience, and some of that is due to incompatibility and our inability to date properly. But I digress…

If we can enter marriage with a "forever" mentality, instead of a "let's just try this" mentality, then we have a large portion of the ingredients needed to make marriage work.

So when you are dating someone, if they are consistently shaky and shady, if they are always threatening to leave you, if they cheat on you, if they lie to you and/or if you wonder if you can trust them, then you are seeing the markings of a bad marriage. Most bad marriages started out as bad relationships; the couple thought that marriage was the solution. But that is not the case. If you are unhappy when you are dating the person, then you are going to be even more unhappy married to them. Marriage just enhances what you already have.

5) Duality of Purpose

When you decide to get married, you are signing up to be more than just one person. You are who you need to be for yourself, but you also are deciding to define yourself based on the opinion of another. If your husband does not like you, then that is a real problem for you as a wife. You can't just say, "Well I think I am great; I think I am a great wife!" Although I understand the desire to feel good about yourself and to defend yourself, you also have to understand that this is a part of the nature of marriage.

You do not get married just to do what you want to do and be who you wanted to be. You should get married because you believe you can be what this person needs you to be.

Moreover, you have to be ready for the duality of your purpose. You can be committed to God, but even God knows that He is going to be sharing you with your spouse and that your interests are divided. You can be committed to your career or your job, but you have to figure out how to be a good lawyer, and a good wife, how to be a good engineer and a good husband, etc. You can be committed to your family and your children, but don't forget your spouse.

If you are not ready to split yourself down the middle, to almost have more than one personality and certainly more than one purpose, then marriage is going be very difficult for you to do.

And when you start to date someone, you are going to be looking for someone who clearly shows you the ability to multitask. You are looking for someone who knows how to prioritize, study, and work, but you're also looking for someone who knows how to make you feel important, unique, and special. If you are dating someone and you already feel ignored or taken for granted, that situation is only going to get worse in a marriage relationship.

Ultimately, dating is supposed to lead to love. I find it fascinating how quickly people will profess love for one another, especially the way love is portrayed in the media. People in the movies on TV fall in and out of love so quickly. You shouldn't be so quick to commit to everlasting, "do-anything-for-you" type of love for a person. Love takes time to develop. And when we are talking about dating love that turns into *marital* love, we are talking about a very unique thing.

Marital, romantic love is not like any other love relationship that we have. We may have seen some aspects of it in our past family experiences, but the sexual component changes the dynamic of the love relationship.

That love needs to be clearly defined.

Romantic Love is...

1) More than a Feeling

Once you get past infatuation, begin to see the real side of the person and decide to stay with them and love them in spite of their shortcomings, you know you really are "in love." As long as you see the person as "perfect," you are not really ready for love.

Maybe a better way to explain it is to say that love covers the faults so that you still see the perfection in the person, in spite of the imperfections that you know are there. Since romantic love is more than a feeling, you decide to continue to love that person, and that is *Real* Love!

2) Stronger than Pride

There is nothing that most people won't do for a love that is reciprocated. Pride can protect you from someone who is just trying to use you, but it can also become a hindrance in a Real Love relationship. Once you have found that person who really loves you, then it is in your best interest to remove all the lines that you have drawn to protect your pride.

Sometimes, when we have been hurt, it can be difficult to trust again. One of the saddest things that I have seen is someone who was more giving to a person who hurt them, rather than the "right" person for them. Many times, men can find themselves carrying the baggage left behind by another man. I have heard people say, "After that, I decided that I would never allow myself to be that vulnerable again."

I understand that pain can make you want to crawl back into your shell. But whether you are a man or a woman, you have to be prepared to move past your negative experiences and open yourself up for the new person who has come along. Make that love stronger than your pride because there is no romantic love without vulnerability.

3) Patient and Forgiving

If you can't let things go from the past, it is going to be even more difficult to let things go in the future. It is like a wastebasket; it has to be emptied regularly. My wife loves cute little trashcans, and I admit that they do fit the décor of the room she is decorating. The problem is that they fill up too quickly. When a tiny, cute bathroom trashcan is full, even a Q-tip will bounce out and end up on the floor. It is not the size of the Q-tip; the problem is the fullness of the can.

In the same way, if I have not dumped the pain from my past, I am not going to be able to deal with any pain or slights that may come in my new relationship, no matter how small they are.

Love requires patience and forgiveness. It is going to take time to get to know one another, and you are going to have to forgive the misunderstandings that take place during the learning curve.

When the person you love says, "I am sorry; I did not know that," then you are going to have to be able to say, "No big deal. We are still learning about one another." Forgiveness is key to the friendship because it is almost impossible to be intimate with someone without pain. The closer we are, the easier it is for us to hurt one another.

4) Trusting and Protecting

In a love relationship, you have to believe the best about the other person. You have to have confidence in their commitment. You can't watch them all the time. You have to believe in what they tell you and trust that they will keep their word.

When you love someone that way, you protect him or her. You cover for him or her; there is privacy in intimacy. So many people violate one another by sharing intimate details and interactions with outsiders. That can be especially damaging when you share hurt and pain caused by the person. When you love someone, the expectation is that you will protect him or her, not expose him or her.

Real Love takes faith. You have to believe in marriage, believe it can work and believe that you won't end up a miserable statistic. You have to believe in the person, believe the best about them and believe that your love can last.

You have to be prepared to defend this person to other people that you love. In-laws become outlaws when they interfere with your relationship. You have to be prepared to deal with your family, and each of you should deal with your own families. Your spouse should not have to get into heated discussions with your family. You take care of your family; you let your mother know that you love her, but things have changed, and she is no longer the priority in your life.

If you are not ready to do that, then marriage is going to be tough to do.

5) Preserving

Real Love lasts. We have to be careful about romantic love because the effects last whether we want them to or not. Think about it for a second. It is easier to get over a person you have not been intimate with. If you are a virgin right now, then, as much as you may have been hurt in a past relationship, that is nothing in comparison to what the pain could have been.

Romantic sex changes us. If we have children as a result, then they are a permanent reminder of a relationship that we had in the past. Something happens when you get under someone else's skin; something happens when you let someone into your body; you get attached to them; life is created; blood is shared. That bond can be difficult to break.

The positive of it is that the bond can be difficult to break. After years of consistent intimacy with one person, you will develop an affinity for them that should not be easy to walk away from. They really will get under your skin, into your heart and into your soul. You will find that it is difficult to live without them; this kind of love perseveres.

And that is why we need to be even more careful about who we create this love with. If you create it with the wrong person, you can find yourself tied to someone who is not right for you.

Dating is not something that we should do recreationally. You ought to know after a few dates whether this person is someone you can see yourself with forever. If forever is not in your future, then start over. Make marriage the goal, and the journey will not be as complicated.

Now that we have defined what marriage is and have determined to make marriage the goal, we can start taking the steps to begin the search.

Chapter 2
Readiness

When you decide that you are ready to start looking, the first person you need to find is yourself. Although some may think that a relationship completes them, in all actuality, you ought to be complete in yourself before you even start dating. We have alluded to this concept already. When you are not healed from past hurts or experiences that can make you focus on yourself first. But when you have forgiven others and yourself—you essentially have let go of your past baggage and are ready for love.

And some of you may even be thinking, "I don't know if I am ready for marriage," or, "I was just looking to date, have some fun, and find some interesting pointers on how to find someone. I am not even sure if I am ready for all of this." And I understand that sentiment. Marriage can be intimidating, especially if we have not seen a good marriage. So many people are coming out of broken homes with parents that got divorced, or even parents that were never married at all. You may not have a whole lot of confidence in your ability to do this "eternal commitment thing."

But the thing about Readiness is that you can actually get ready. There are things that you can do to get ready, things to work on so that you can be a complete person. *Real Love* is about giving, not getting. If you want to be a giver, then there are some traits you will have to have and some work that you will have to do.

Maybe you aren't ready. But a lot of times, people are just making excuses to avoid commitment. So lets define Readiness.

Reasons You May Not be Ready

1) Not in Love with Yourself

It is very difficult to have someone else love you when/if you don't love yourself. You are going to treat other people the way you want to be treated. That is the golden rule: "To do unto others as you would have them do unto you." But if your standards for yourself are not that high, then you are not going to treat another person very well.

When you look at yourself, you have to like what you see. It is called *self-esteem.* Too many people find all of their value and self-worth in the eyes of another person. Although you are doing your best to please this person, at the same time, you have to have a sense of yourself. You have to know who you are and like what you see.

And if not, then make the changes now. Don't wait until you meet that person and then join a gym to get in shape for them. Get in shape for *yourself.* Look good for *you*; love *yourself.* If you don't love you, how can I love you?

2) Not Old Enough–Too Young

Obviously, someone who is only in high school is not ready to be married. And I know that there are high school sweethearts out there, people who have been together forever and have a great relationship. You can change a lot between the ages of eighteen and twenty-two, and you want to make sure that physical connection has not blinded you into obvious incompatibility. We have to be careful, for it is even more likely for people to grow out of the relationship with one another during this stage of life.

There are some exceptions, but really, once you are past twenty-one, it is time to get serious about looking. I know some people may think that twenty-two is young for marriage, but you want to be careful not to wait too long. The older you get, the more careful you get, and the more particular you get. There are positives and negatives in that. You are more careful, so you are less likely to make a foolish mistake. But at the same time, a love relationship is always a chance, and sometimes people get so careful that it is difficult for them to take the plunge.

Also, as you age, you get more set in your ways. You are a bit more flexible when you are younger. It is easier to grow together, and you are not so stuck on any particular method of doing something. Marriage needs flexibility; you want to be able to adapt to each other.

Also, there is a set time when women can have children easily and healthily. You want to be able to be married for a few years before children enter the picture; you will need that time to form the appropriate bonds to survive the challenge of childbirth and family. So, the sooner you can settle down, the more time you will have to actually learn one another, grow together, and even save some money to be prepared for a family.

If you are reading this and you are twenty-two or older, it is time to get serious.

3) No Mission, No Job, No Direction

You need to have a plan for your life. You are looking for someone who can come alongside of you and help you with your goals in life. How can you find that woman if you do not know what you are going to do? If you are going to be a doctor, then you need a spouse who can handle the schooling, hours, and work required to make you successful. If you are in the military and that is going to be your career, you need someone who is ready for that particular unique sacrifice.

Ultimately, I am saying: you need to know where you are going. Actually, you should be on your way there so that this person you will meet will be someone who is on their way to their own destiny. If they are on the way, then they probably are heading in a similar direction.

This can be particularly tough for women, though, because a man can change everything. You want to be strong, determined and driven, but if you are going to have a husband, you are going to have to be ready for change. My suggestion is that you make your plans in pencil, not in pen. You may be planning on going to law school in New York, but if you meet a man who has a career in Georgia, your plans may have to change.

Actually, this can apply to both people. The important thing is to make that relationship a priority. Finding the person to spend the rest of your life with is much harder than finding a job or a good graduate program. If you want Real Love, then love has to be moved higher in your priorities. Just as you went after that career, that degree, that promotion, you are going to have to pursue, and be ready to sacrifice for a good relationship.

4) Not Healthy

Marriage and relationships are hard work. It is going to be even more difficult to do if you are not healthy. If you have physical issues, I would suggest that you move past your issues before seeking a relationship. It can be a lot to ask another person to deal with your sickness while trying to get to know you. I know that this can sound harsh, but ask yourself if it is really fair for you to ask someone to be saddled with your disease? Will you really be able to give all that you can while battling sickness? Love is about giving.

If you have mental issues going in, that situation needs to be dealt with as well. If you are not healed from past hurts, still dealing with un-forgiveness, and/ or wrestling with trauma from your childhood, that can be tough for a spouse to deal with. For example, if you were molested as a child and have sexual hang-ups and baggage as a result of it, I would suggest that you get counsel and be healed of that past trauma. I don't think it is fair to ask someone you love to deal with the after-effects of the damage that was done to you.

That difficulty will always be a part of you, and a person who loves you will love you in spite of what you went through. But you have to move past it enough to be healthy and functional. You can't be a bad parent just because you had bad parents. You can't abuse just because you were abused. Come to grips with your issues; deal with what was done to you; get help and move forward, then you will be healthy, whole, and ready to meet someone.

5) Not Ready to Work – Lazy

Marriage, Relationships and Family, these are work words. It all requires a significant amount to work. There is nothing worse than a lazy spouse. You have to be prepared to do the work that relationship requires. You know you are mature when you do the work that needs to be done, not just what you feel like doing.

And we have specific roles that we have to play. The work is not all the same. We are equal, but we are not the same; we are looking for different things.

To be a good wife there are many things that you are going to have to do well. I want to focus on three of them: they are what I call, *The Three S's:* Sex, Slack, and Silence.

Sex – Men are looking for *sex*; women are looking for romance. And men exchange romance for sex. So be prepared: when a man does something romantic, he usually has sex in mind.

When I say *sex*, I don't just mean lying there, but knowing how to work the equipment, knowing how to enjoy sex, and knowing how to respond, move, and even initiate. You have to know how to be alluring, desirable, and sexy. If you marry a normal, healthy, fully heterosexual man, you are going to need to be ready to have sex, and lots of it.

When we are talking about sex, we are also talking about attraction. Men are into the physical. Men are visual. They want to be attracted to, and want to stay attracted to, their woman.

Slack – Men are always looking for *Slack*. Slack is your ability to cut him a break when he is not perfect. A man will give flowers to make up for a mistake. A man will give a gift in the hopes that it will make you say, "Well, he left hair in the sink, but at least he bought me this bracelet." That is Slack, and all men are looking for it.

Silence – Men love peace and quiet. Women have more words than men. The average woman speaks about 25,000 words a day, while men average about 12,000. So at the end of any given day, a man can be almost talked out. We know that you love communication, but sometimes, just sit there and be "eye candy;" that is a valuable skill.

Talking is great, but a man does not want to talk all the time. And when men communicate, it is with a solution in mind. We talk to give and find answers. If you just want to chat, without judgment or solution, then we may not be the best ones to talk to all the time.

A man is not really all that interested in your problems. He wants a woman who is happy, healthy, and horny. I don't mean to be crude, but that is what we are looking for: someone who has herself together, is ready to serve at any moment, and can bring home the bacon and fry it up in that pan while never letting me forget I am a man; *a woman.*

Now I have some *S's* for the guys as well. Gentlemen, if you are going to be a good husband, you are going to have to do these three S's well: *Security, Sympathy, and Sensitivity.*

Security – Ever had a woman ask you if you would stay with her even if she lost her arms and legs? What if she got burned up in a fire? What if she got big like her momma? Would you still love her? They ask those questions because they don't want to be abandoned. They want to feel as if you are going to be there for the long haul.

They don't want to be threatened every time you get upset. They want to know that the relationship is secure, that the home is secure. They want to know that the bills are paid that you didn't forget what they asked you to do. You are going to have to be ready to be consistent, to be trustworthy, to be easily found and easily trustable.

They want to get married to make a commitment. They have a certain amount of patience, but they want to know where this relationship is going. What are the long-term plans? They want to know that there is a future.

Sympathy – Women like to communicate, not just to get an answer or a solution. They want agreement; they want to know that you identify with them, that you think they are right, that you sympathize with their plight.

This can be tough because we are not women, and we don't think as they do. But they want to communicate as though we have more in common, rather than less in common. Women like to focus on the ways that we are compatible. Your ability to understand them is very important to a woman. She does not want to be a mystery to you. Women are not like us; we are testers. Women will give you a test and then give you the book and the answers to the test, then will look over your shoulder while you take it and help you fill it out. They need to feel understood.

Sensitivity – This can be one of the toughest for us. Women want to be able to depend on the robot inside you. Good men are like Cyborgs: flesh on the outside but steel within. There is nothing wrong with being a Cyborg as long as you have the right programmer. She wants to be able to depend on the robot on the inside, but she doesn't want to live and sleep with metal and wire.

They want an emotional connection; they are looking for romantic gestures, words, flowers and gifts. They think about how much time you have spent together. When was the last time you really talked to her, opened up to her? They want your intimacy to be relational, not just physical.

Women want to know that we have feelings; they want to know when we are hurt. They want us to share our fears with them, our disappointments. And that is just not how most of us were raised. Men are raised to be tough, to keep moving, to be strong and silent. That is our goal.

Women understand that, but they don't want us to be cold, hard and uncaring. They want to hear, "I love you." They want to believe that we need hugs, not just for sex. They want a certain amount of sensitivity.

So you can't be Lazy; you have to be ready to *work* and *work hard*. Relationships are *work*.

6) Not Open

If you are too closed off and/or not ready to listen and learn, you are not ready for a relationship. Real Love is like going back to school. You have to be ready to learn about the person; learn what they like and don't like. If you are not ready to open up and share your heart and your feelings, then you are not ready. No one can ready your mind, you have to be ready to teach and learn.

Every person is different. Even with this book, I can give you some good, general information, but no one can teach you to be a good spouse like the person you marry. In a way, you are looking for their job description. When he thinks "wife" what comes to mind? When she thinks "husband," what is her definition?

When you are open, you are ready to change, ready to adapt. True strength is seen in flexibility, not rigidity. If you are not ready to be open to growing and being flexible, then you are not ready for love.

Also, when I say, "open," I mean Open, like a business. Always be approachable; don't adopt a philosophy where you can't meet anyone right now. Just because you have been hurt does not mean you should close your store. No one is saying you have to be vulnerable; you don't have to take them into the kitchen and show them your secret recipes, but fix up the dining area and get back open for business. Don't let a storm close your store. You don't want to be closed when the right "customer" comes along.

7) Not a Giver

Marriage is about selflessness. That would be the seventh "S" if I were making that list. *Sex, Slack, Silence, Security, Sympathy, Sensitivity,* and *Selflessness.* Love is not for selfish people. The idea is to put the needs of another above your own. When you put your significant other's needs first and he/she puts your needs first as well, both of your individual needs will be met.

But if you are just looking out for you, and he/she is just looking out for himself/herself, you will find yourselves fighting for what you each need. Once you find someone who has the ability to meet your needs, once you find that special one that has everything you need on your list, the next question is—"Can you match that?" Can you give on the same level that they can give?

One of the ironies of relationships is that there are great people mixed up with terrible people. Allow me to explain. Most relationships fall into one of these 3 categories.

1) Both people are terrible, crazy, shouldn't be married. This group makes up about twenty-five percent of the people who are married. Both people are selfish, takers, rude, not able to love right and not able to be faithful and consistent.

2) Both people are great. This group makes up about twenty-five percent of the people who are married. This is the group I am trying to get you into. You both are givers, faithful, mature and healthy; you love one another, you are great friends and are compatible.

3) One person is great; the Other person is not. Unfortunately, in my experience, this group makes up about fifty percent of married people. In many problematic marriages, there is one person who really needs the help. The other person would probably be happily married if they had married better.

It is tough to be happy in a marriage when you are loving, faithful, consistent, and sane; yet you are married to a crazy, inconsistent, unfriendly, non-communicative jerk.

You want to find someone as wonderful as you. When both people are givers, marriage is not as difficult.

All of these concepts will prepare you to be ready to date. Now I trust that I have not totally scared you away from dating and marriage, for this is only Chapter 2. Fortunately, as I said earlier, you can get ready. Do the work.

It doesn't make sense to find the perfect person if you are just going to mess it up with your craziness and insecurity. Get Healthy! Then you will be Ready.

Chapter 3
The Search

Once you are Ready, then the search can begin. Love is something you find. You are not going to just stumble into it; it will not take you by surprise. You are going to have to put forth some effort to find fulfilling love. You are going to have to be intentional.

That is one of the reasons God put you in a love relationship from birth; you were not hatched in an egg and left on your own. We are born helpless, utterly dependent on people who are supposed to love and care for us. And you did not even realize it, but while caring for you, your parents were teaching you about love.

And I trust that they taught you well. Unfortunately, some of us have a "love compass" that is off. Our parents messed us up; we had a father that abandoned us and/ or an overly possessive mother. We had a dad who was unreasonable, so now we see men as unreasonable; we had a mother that lied a lot, so we think all women lie. Those lessons were important. In case you did not learn right, or even if you did but did not realize it, let me outline what parental love was supposed to teach you.

Parental love was supposed to be...

1) Sacrificial – Your parents were supposed to put your needs above their own. You were supposed to be the priority. You did not ask to be born. They were not supposed to bring you into this world because they were lonely and looking for a really good friend.

We did not notice it at the time, but now, those of us who are parents realize just how much that sacrifice was. You mother's body changed for you; she went sleepless for months for you, changed you diaper more times than she could count—actually wiped feces from your backside—took you to the doctor, took you to your practices for whatever you were doing, went to the recitals and plays that you were terrible in and then told you that you were good when everyone knew you weren't.

She sacrificed!

And your dad did some of that stuff. Mostly, his sacrifice was having your mother less, but you get my point. They sacrificed.

Wait a minute! Dads do sacrifice in a huge way. Dads get up in the middle of the night, too, take you to practice, go to your games, sit on hard bleachers for hours at a time, let you have pets that they can't stand and listen to you screaming for no good reason. You get my point: the love was sacrificial.

They were supposed to be prepared for the responsibility of parenting so that they could make the necessary sacrifice so that you could have the best they could provide.

2) Dependable – They were supposed to be trustworthy. You weren't supposed to wonder if they were going to come get you. They were supposed to keep their word. Their integrity was something that you were supposed to be able to depend on. In fact, you should have been so dependable that you had to be taught to say thank you. You just expected juice; at one point, you started to just say, "Juice!" with the expectation that a Sippy cup would magically appear in your hand. It was your mother who said, "Juice, WHAT," which prompted you to say, "Please?" That happened because that love was so dependable that you almost took it for granted.

But that is what love is supposed to be: so dependable that you have to remind yourself to say, "Thank you." And when you express the gratitude, the person should almost have an attitude, as if to say, "But that is what I am supposed to do; you don't have to thank me for that; this is love."

After 18 years with your parents, you were supposed to believe that love and trust went hand in hand. It was supposed to help you to know that you are supposed to be dependable and that you should be looking for someone who could be trusted.

3) Life-Sustaining–That love sustained your life. You couldn't really take care of yourself for the first eighteen years of your life. That love fed you, put a roof over your head, helped you with homework, drove you everywhere, picked you up, and reminded

you of your responsibilities. You would not be alive today without love.

It was not promised one minute and then denied the next minute. It kept going until you could take care of yourself. If you ended up on your own at thirteen, just realize that even though you made it, that that was not how life was supposed to be. Maybe you are unable to form lasting, loving relationships because you became so self-sustaining that you no longer need anyone. Understand why it happened, but also realize that you did not learn the real lesson of *Real Love*.

4) Behavior-Correcting – You may have been raised by parents who did not have a very serious standard for your behavior. Maybe you were allowed to do whatever you wanted. That is a dangerous lesson because everything has consequences. And real love will correct you. If you are not open to being corrected by love, then you may be surprised when the person you love has to confront you. Just because I love you does not mean that you are perfect.

Real love should help me be better, just like that love from your parents. It made you grow. Good parents will love you, just the way you are, but thankfully they loved you too much to leave you the way you were. You needed correction. Where would you be if your parents "broke up" with you for saying, "No" for the first time? Where would you be if their response had been, "You know, this is just not working out for me. I have known you for these two years that you have been alive, and it has been tough, but now you are doing some things, and I just don't know if I can continue in this relationship..." That would have been insane; you were two, in your "terrible two's."

But that is not what they did. They corrected you; they helped you be better; they instructed you on how to walk, how to clean and ultimately how to live with them. And in that same manner, Real Love helps me to be better. I am a better man today. After more than two decades together, nearly twenty-five years, my wife has changed me, and I have changed her. Some of that came through time, familiarity, but quite a bit of it came through correction.

My point is that parental love was supposed to set within you a definition of love that became instinct in your search for love. You were supposed to be able to recognize it, like a fragrance that is pleasing. If you went to a perfume store and a salesperson tried to sell you a fragrance that smelled like bad fish with a hint of dog breath, you would not buy it. As soon as the salesperson sprayed it on that tiny piece of paper and waved it in front of your nose, you would ask for something different.

In that same way, love without sacrifice stinks. Love without correction smells weird. Love that is not dependable has a weird odor. And there are many of us who know that since we have had "fake love" waved in front of our faces before, we know what it smells like—fish and dog.

The love we search for should be better that parental love. It should reflect it, but it should be an upgrade.

That Real Love ought to enhance my life. I should want to see the person, look forward to hearing their voice, want to talk to them and let them know what I am doing, where I am, when I will be home. That love says, "Sure I'll come get you. Sure, I can drive you to work. You need a sandwich? No problem; I got you!" This love should sustain your life. Life ought to get better and better with love.

And that is why God put you in a family. He has put you in a family so that when it comes time to choose the person that you are going to create family with, you will have seen the blueprint so that you can find someone with the raw qualities needed to create good family.

So where do you begin?

Misconceptions

Before we actually get stared, I think it would be wise to first do away with all of the wrong ideas, misconceptions and insane advice from ignorant friends, which can impede us in this process.

1) It Will Just Happen One Day / God is Going to Choose this Person for Me

As I stated earlier, Men, you are going to have to *find* a wife! You are going to have to take the time to search. I don't want to beat the point to death, but it takes intentionality. If you are not intentional, something may happen, but it may not be what you want. Someone may come along, but that may end up being more painful than pleasant.

And we are going to talk about this in subsequent chapters, but let me just mention it quickly here. If you are a woman, you definitely have to be intentional. I am not saying "chase men," but you don't have time to waste either. The energy you gave to pursuing a career is going to have to be matched by the attention you give to developing a relationship.

Some Christians want to put it all on God, but dude, God is not putting any more men to sleep, taking a rib out and creating a woman for them. That was a one-shot deal. Woman, you are not going to wake up one day and hear God say, "Here's your Adam!"

You are going to have to be prepared to do some work! Many Christians love to blame God for their relationships: "Well, this is who God told me to marry." But there is no Bible for that sentiment. There is not one place anywhere in the Bible where God tells anyone to marry anyone.

I believe in trusting God. Trust that He will guide you, direct you and correct you. Believe He will bring clarity. He will help you when you start to make a list. He will speak to you about yourself, and begin to instruct you on how to be prepared.

But He is not going to "choose" the person for you. You have free will. The choice is still up to you.

If you "fall" in love, you may break something; you may hurt yourself. I suggest you open your eyes and look before you leap. Step into love with some sense.

2) Perfection

There is no such thing as a perfect woman or a perfect man. The question is not, "Are they perfect?"

Even if you were to find the perfect person, you would mess them up because you are far from perfect. None of us are perfect.

The question is, "Are they perfect for me?" That is what you are looking for, someone who fits with you and your perfections and imperfections, the yin to your yang, that person who brings balance to your life.

There is no such thing as a perfect relationship. If I have perfection as the goal for my relationship, then I am going to be disappointed most of the time. You can have a very good relationship and an excellent marriage. But even excellent marriages are likely to have tough times in them. And when the tough times come, that is when you get to find out how good your marriage really is. It is not a very good one if perfection in every situation is a requirement for commitment. I am far from perfect, but my wife is still here because we have a great relationship. She is not perfect, but I stick around because we are right for each other. Together, we strive to be the best that we can be for each other. The good outweighs the bad.

3) We Should be Exactly Alike

When Paula Abdul recorded the song "Opposites Attract," she stumbled onto a concept that actually has some validity. I don't know if I would go so far as to say that opposites "should" attract. I recognize that they often do attract, and that can be good and bad. Too much "opposite" can be a disruptive factor in your relationship. If you are faithful and committed, you do not want to find the "opposite" of that, unfaithful and promiscuous. If you are good with money, you should not be looking for the "opposite," little Miss Spend-it-all. If you are neat, you do not want to be with someone who is a slob. Opposites can work, but there are limits. You should not be totally opposite in order to be together, but you don't have to be exactly the same either.

My wife and I were at dinner, and I was talking to her about this point that I was going to make in this book. To test my concept, we did a little exercise in which we listed what we had in common, and then compared that list to our differences. We were surprised to find that we did not share as much in common as we originally believed. We just knew when we started that we were going to be the same. We just knew that we were going to "debunk" the idea that opposites attract. But we found out we were wrong.

Now I am not trying to hold us up as the perfect couple, but we have been married since 1991. So you do the math. We get along; we love each other, and we like each other. But we are very different. She is a morning person; I am a night person. She reads because she needs to, and mostly reads non-fiction. I was an English major; I read all the time, and fiction to me is life. She was great at science; she is a detail-oriented person. I tolerated science and focused on the big picture. She loves variety; she loves to try new things, new places to eat and new cuisine. I tend to do the same things all the time. I will eat at the same restaurant and order the same thing every time I go there. I grew up the oldest of eight children. My parents were married in 1967, and they are still together. She has never met her father; she is the younger of two children, raised by a single mother, and for a while, a single aunt.

You get the point; we are very different. We found that the key to our relationship was "Compromise." I am sure that there are many couples that would find that this is the case. Compatibility does not mean absolute similarity.

Actually, you would be wise to find someone who has strengths where you may have some weaknesses. If you are an introvert, the last thing you need to do is get involved with another introvert. If you like to talk all the time, you may need to find someone who really likes to listen. Do not look for your twin; look for someone who not only fits your present but also your future.

4) Love is a Feeling

Certainly love is an emotion that we feel. But love is such a broad idea; it cannot be simply defined as a feeling. The bigger issue is that ascribing love to the feeling category leaves too much room for the weakness of human whimsy. If love is only a feeling, then it is hard to connect it to a word like "forever"; but that is how we refer to it today. Too many people use "feeling" as an excuse to go back on promises made. They will say, "I fell out of love with them," or "I just don't think I love them anymore."

So when we talk about Real Love, we have to narrow that definition. What we describe as that "feeling" of love is better defined as infatuation. The butterflies-in-the-stomach and the leaping of the heart within the chest feelings are important parts of the beginning of a relationship, but they are not the glue that creates commitment. Real Love begins when you see the attributes in the person that may not be so wonderful, yet you decide to love them in spite of their imperfections. Love is a commitment to endure every challenge that we may face.

As we said earlier, it is reminiscent of the love we experienced from our parents. Your mother's love was more than a feeling; it was something that could never be shaken. It is what the world needs to see: real people who love each other, forever.

Now that takes the search task to another level. I hope these first few chapters have not scared you away from this book. You may have thought this was going to be a manual on dating, or maybe some quick pointers on how to meet women. And, hey, I am willing to give you some pointers. I am not afraid to give advice. God knows I have an opinion; that is why I wrote this book. I just want to make sure that we understand the task that we face. Dating can be fun until someone gets hurt. If you have the right focus and the right technique is used, you can enjoy the ride without falling out of the rollercoaster.

So here are some tips, and they will apply to both sexes.

Tips as you start the search

1) Value Yourself – I know we talked about this a bit in "Readiness," but it bears repeating. Know yourself; like yourself; value Yourself. Understand that you are unique; there is no one like you. No one has your DNA or fingerprints; you are one of a kind!

   Man, have confidence in yourself. Confidence is very attractive. And since we value respect, you want to find someone who is attracted to confidence. You don't have to look like Brad Pitt or Denzel Washington to get a wonderful woman. You are a valuable and unique commodity.

   Woman, you have to know who you are. You do not have to be Halle Berry. You do not have to be Angelina Jolie or Salma Hayak. Be the best you can be, and value yourself. The standard of self-confidence is attractive.

2) Look in the Right Place – If you want a booty call, go to the club. If you want someone you can introduce to your parents, you may have to change where you look: maybe go to a church event or a gathering at a friend's house. Also, keep your eyes open when you are on campus. If you want an educated man, you need to try to find one when you are still in school. If you want a woman with integrity, you may not want to talk to one who has a reputation for "sleeping" around.

   I know I am being extreme, but you get the point. If I want good seafood, I go to a city that is near the ocean. I don't go to Texas for great seafood. I go to Texas if I want a good steak.

3) Get Clean – Bathe, dress nicely, do your hair, get a haircut and don't be lazy.

4) Never turn down an opportunity – even if you just broke up with someone and you feel as if you are still "healing." If the right person comes along, heal quickly. Don't turn down someone better because of the last loser who hurt you. If the upgrade comes, take the upgrade. I am not saying rush into anything new. If you need to heal, then heal; just don't be a slow healer.

5) Believe that it is possible. I know I have said that before, but it is true. If you lose hope, you will reek either of desperation or hopelessness. Keep the faith; keep your head up. If at first you don't succeed, brush yourself off, and try again.

Chapter 4

Have You Seen Her?

G entlemen, so much is on us as men. It is tough to avoid the blame for a failing relationship. When you begin to understand the magnitude of the task that lies ahead, it will either scare you to death or inspire you to action. My desire is that you be inspired.

And let's be honest. Sex is a huge factor for us as men. It is one of the strongest drives we have, trumped only by the drive to breathe, live, and eat. Once we reach puberty, our bodies start us on this search. But sex is not supposed to be the primary goal, but rather the jeweled crown that sits on the head of the relationship's body. Sex is something that we all seek; but if you are not careful, that very drive that was meant to bring you life can ironically kill your future.

Once you understand that you are walking a fine line between life and death, the gravity of this choice is unavoidable. And sometimes, the more options you have, the more daunting the task of choosing someone. In most cultures, men have the power of choice. Because we have that power, we also have to shoulder the majority of the responsibility.

As a man, you have to be ready to accept the blame. What I am saying is that if your marriage fails, it is your fault. I know you may be able to point out all the flaws of the woman you are with, and I am sure she is flawed. There is no such thing as a perfect woman, or man, for that matter. But even if she is terrible, you are the one who chose her. You walked up to her; you asked her out; you asked her to marry you.

I know that social norms have changed some, and women are asking men out in recent times. But I have never heard of a woman asking a man to marry her. That question will always be yours to ask. If you had never asked her to marry you, you wouldn't be married.

If you were "guilted" into marriage or forced into it because of a pregnancy, well, that is still your fault. As men, our seed is the most valuable thing that we have. We actually have the power to create life. But we do not treat that seed as valuable. We will give it to anyone that wants it.

And that is why we get ourselves into trouble. It is like shopping. No matter where you shop, Best Buy, Home Depot, Target, or Wal-Mart, the people who run the store know how to put products in front of you to attract your attention. Stores make money on "Impulse Shopping." You may go in to buy a loaf of bread or a gallon of milk, but that is not in the front of the store. That is in the back of the store so that you will have to walk through all the "Impulse Buys." You might go into the store for milk, but walk out with "buy-one-get-one-free" items.

When my mother taught me to shop, she taught me to go into a store with a list, and to only get the things on the list. She taught me to bring only enough money for the things on my list. She never imagined the invention of the check card, where you have all of your money that is in the bank in your wallet at one time. With a list and a limited amount of money, it is more difficult to "Impulse Shop."

And gentlemen, that is what I am trying to help you to avoid: "Impulse Shopping." You are looking for bread and milk, but some Fruit Loops may walk by, which prompts you to chase cereal. What you need is a Salad and a good meal, but you end up chasing after junk.

I trust you realize I am not talking about food. There are too many of us who think candy is food. There is more to a good woman than just hips, breasts, and legs, not to say that those things are not important. But it is possible to find food that is good for you and tastes good.

More to the point, I'm saying that it is possible to find a good woman who also looks good. I know that we are motivated by sight, and there is nothing wrong with that. You just need to avoid the "Impulse Buy." Find a good woman by sticking to a prepared list and a strict "budget."

It is going to be a challenge; especially since our world and our current 21st century culture is determined to glorify the power of "Impulse Shopping." We admire guys who can pick up a woman in a bar and sleep with her right away. We say that those men have "game." We call them smooth, suave, ladies' men. I call them reckless, walking on the edge of danger. Is it any wonder that so many children are born into homes without fathers and that 50% of marriages are ending in divorce?

We have turned into "Impulse Shoppers." But if we can break that cycle, then we can actually find what we are looking for. And the way to do that is to use the exact strategies that my mother taught me. Make a List, and Have a Limit.

Making a List

The beginning of making a list is the knowledge that you need to make one. I can give you instruction, but much of that will be general, because as men, we are all different; we are looking for different things. Thankfully, we share enough in common so that I can advise you. But understand, your list will look a bit different from that of another man.

I have four brothers. We have the same parents and were raised in the same home and city. We share so much in common, and we are all married. But if you were to meet all of our wives, you would see five totally different women. One of the wives is from a foreign country; some are short, and some are tall. There are things that they have in common, and they are all great women. But my point is made. When we made our lists, there were some things that the lists had in common, but then there were many differences as well.

I want to focus on what we have in common, what we as good men are looking for in a good woman. Just understand that this will be a skeleton to your own personal list, the beginning of helping you create a list. But it is not the "Bible" of a good woman.

The List

1) Similar

It should be easy to have things in common. Agreement is the foundation of any good relationship. So it does not make sense trying to be with someone who is absolutely nothing like you.

If you are spiritual and believe in God, then she needs to be spiritual and believe in God.

If you are a dog lover, she needs to like dogs.

If you love the outdoors, it would be good if she likes the outdoors.

If you love to stay home, then it would be good if she is a "home body" too.

If you love the movies, dinner out, vacations on the beach, bike riding or whatever, you need to start with some good similarities. People will change, but she shouldn't have to change everything about herself just to be with you. She may not love football the way that you do, she may not love everything you love. But she can't hate it either.

Although opposites attract, there is a limit to how far that can stretch, before you are dealing with factors that can make you have a bad relationship.

2) Attractive

Obviously, we are men. We are motivated by sight. So you need to find a woman that is attractive to you. You should want her physically and like what you see when you look at her. She needs to look good, even when she is not at her best. When she gets "made-up," the cosmetics should just enhance a beauty that you already see.

It's like ice cream. I like ice cream already; it is good just the way it is. If you cut a banana in half, put the scoops of ice cream on top of it and then add some hot fudge, some whipped cream, and some almonds, I will be even happier. I love a good banana split. But ice cream in a bowl sounds good to me, too. She needs to at least be ice cream in a bowl.

The make up, the clothes, lingerie, hairstyles, etc., all need to be the hot fudge and the whipped cream. She needs to look good enough to the point where she is fine just in a bowl.

There are a lot of men who have compromised attraction for other qualities. Although that is admirable, it has led many to disaster. A woman needs to be wanted and she needs to look good to you for her own sake. You are not doing a woman any favors by being with her if you do not find her desirable. You need to like what you see; she should turn you on.

3) Nice and Sweet

I am not saying she should be a pushover, but you need to find someone who knows how to treat you right. I am always amazed when I hear about some guy getting in trouble for abusing his woman. First, a guy should have enough sense to know better; and if he is dealing with mental issues that cause him to want to batter a helpless female, then he needs to get some counseling so that he won't be involved in such destructive behavior again.

But let's say she is not so helpless. Although there is never a good reason to strike a woman, there are women who will challenge you, get in your face, treat you so disrespectfully, and belittle you to a point where you are angry enough to be violent. And I can't understand why a man, someone who has the power of choice, would put himself in that situation.

Whenever I see a man with a wife who is rude, disrespectful, mouthy and mean, I just shake my head. That did not start after marriage. I know sometimes the media tries to paint wives with that brush, as if all wives are mean, spiteful nags, but that generalization is not always the case.

A woman who is mean to you and rude to you as your wife, was more than likely rude, mean, and mouthy when you were dating. No man wants to come home to complaining and brow beating. So don't even put yourself in that situation. Find someone who knows how to talk to you, someone who knows how to be nice and sweet.

4) Happy

Along those same lines, you want a happy woman. There is nothing worse than a constantly depressed, bitter woman. You should not have to be the only thing that brings her joy. She should know how to be happy, even when she is by herself. Believe me, if she does not know how to be content when she is alone, you are not going to be able to make her happy.

As men, we are not that interested in women's problems. We will listen for a bit, then try to give a solution in the hopes that she will feel better so that we can go back to being happy. We are not interested in someone who cannot be appeased, not matter what we do or say. If you allow your life to get tied to an unhappy woman, eventually, you will start looking for someone who is a "fun" girl, someone who knows how to laugh, someone who likes to have a good time. But that person ought to be your wife. And if you pick well, then she will be.

5) Healthy

Being a wife is hard work. As men, we are looking for everything. We want it all. We want someone who is smart, someone who works hard, is a good mother, and is still sexy. That takes energy. A woman needs to be healthy if she is going to be able to do the work that will be required. I am not saying that someone who is disabled or has an illness cannot be a good wife. But there will be limitations to what she can provide, and you both will have to understand that going in.

You want someone who is tough, or what we call a "ride or die chick"; someone you know will stick with you through the tough times and is unbreakable. Life can be full of challenges, and you want a woman who will not shrink back from a fight. She needs to be ready to fight for you and with you, not someone who just wants to fight against you.

So not only will she need to be physically healthy, but even more importantly, she will need to be mentally healthy. She needs to have a good outlook on life and needs to be able to have a rational conversation. Some men think that all women are crazy, but that is not the case. It is true that women are wired a bit differently than we are and can be more emotional. But that is a far step from crazy.

She needs to have a healthy attitude about the things that will be required of her to be a good wife. If she has an unhealthy attitude about sex, submission, agreement, or any of the concepts that you see as important, then I would suggest you continue your search.

You can hear her attitude just by listening to her talk. If she says things like "Who said you are in charge?" or "Why do we always have to do what you want?" or "This is my money, and I am going to do with it what I want," you need to keep searching. Any negative attitude is a sign of real problems that lie ahead. If you believe that you are supposed to be a leader, then you need to avoid rebels at all costs.

Some women live with a perpetual chip on their shoulders. It is almost as if they are angry about being a woman and are always complaining about fairness and equality. I am not saying things should not be fair and equal. Women should have equal rights and equal pay for the same work. I am just saying that you don't want to end up with a woman who secretly resents you just because you are a man. A real woman has to embrace being a woman, in spite of the challenges that womanhood may bring.

6) Smart / Wise

Also, you want a woman who has some sense. Someone who knows how to think and can keep her head in a tough situation is invaluable. And it is even better if she knows some things that you may not know. Just because you are the man does not mean that you have to have all the answers. She will enhance your life significantly if she has brains in her head.

She needs to know how to apply the knowledge that she has. A wise woman understands men, and instead of complaining about them uses the information to her advantage. That is wisdom.

You are not going to want to communicate with someone you think is dumb; that is going to be a real problem for her. A woman wants to communicate, but if you are bored by her conversation, then you will want to avoid it. She needs to be interesting, and she needs to be able to understand you when you are talking. She may not be educated in your field of expertise, but she needs to be able to at least grasp a concept that you are trying to explain.

7) Open

She should be ready for change and open to new experiences. She may think she knows you and what you want, but she needs to be prepared for the fact that you may want more than she expected.

This is especially important when it comes to your sexual relationship. You want a woman who is open, or what I call a "yes girl." There are three types of women who get married:

"No" Women – these are women who are never all that interested in sex; their first response to anything sexual is fear, fatigue, or uninterested acceptance. They say, "yes" as long as it is over quickly. They make a man feel as if he is "doing his business" to them. They are basically the women who either need to get counsel, or never should have been married in the first place.

"Got to Have it" Women – there are some women who are more interested in sex than even men are. These

women are rare, but they do exist. The only challenge with them is that they can make you wonder if they are hot for you or just hot for "it." But if you can find a woman like this, who still has all the other qualities of a good woman, she is a rare and valuable wife.

"Yes" Women – I think most good wives fall into this category. They may not have been thinking about sex at that moment, but when approached, their initial response is "yes." They are open to new things and determined to be who you need them to be sexually; they have a desire for you to be happy.

If you can find a good woman, someone open to learning who you are and what moves you, that is a wonderful thing. Let's be honest; a physical relationship is one of the forces that drives us to commitment. Marriage can be hard work, but the blessing of a fulfilling physical relationship makes the sacrifice seem small.

Gentlemen, you are going to have to be careful. We all want to have power, to be strong like Sampson, but we have to avoid the "Delilahs" that are out there. Unfortunately, there are a lot of women who want to get married for all the wrong reasons. They think they are in love, but their love is misguided.

Some Women Marry Because...

A) They love themselves
B) They love the idea of marriage
C) They love what marriage and a husband can do for them
D) And then, finally, hopefully, they love you.

But that is not what you want; you want a woman who loves you first. She loves you so much that she does not care about a ring; she does not care where you get married as long as she gets to marry you. When you find someone like that, you know you have found a good woman; you have found a "good thing."

The Limit

The other strategy my mother taught me to avoid, along with "Impulse Shopping," was *The Limit*. If you use cash and have only a set amount to spend, then it is difficult to impulse buy things that you do not need.

In that same way, there need to be some limits or restrictions that you put on yourself to help you to find the right woman for you. We will expound on these ideas in more detail when we talk about how to date, but this is a good place to introduce some of these ideas.

As men, we will take whatever we can get if there are no limitations. The idea that we will "never buy the cow if we get the milk for free" is a concept that is founded upon the truth about us. There needs to be a limit to keep us from taking advantage. There was a time when women provided that limitation. But as the morality of our culture has gotten more lax, women have become less likely to make demands and hold to a standard. It is not as easy to hold on to the value of something you have when every other woman is giving hers away. A woman with integrity and a strong sense of herself can often find herself alone in this loose climate we live in.

My point is that if there is going to be a standard and limitations, we may have to supply them for ourselves. Here are a few for you to consider.

1) One Woman at a Time – It is hard enough to choose, without juggling two or three women at once. If you think you have found a good woman, have the sense and the decency to give her your undivided attention as you look to see if she is your match.

2) Four dates – If you are going to buy a car, you should have done your research before you walked onto the lot. If you know you want a BMW, you shouldn't have to test drive the car ninety times before you are ready to buy it. If you are not there to buy, then you are wasting the dealer's time.

In the same way, how many dates do you require before you know if you want to see her again? If you have done your homework, made a list, checked her out and watched her a bit, then you ought to know a bit already. The more dates you take her on without being serious, the more you are wasting her time. Don't be cruel. If she talks too much for you, you are going to know that before date four.

3) Six months – In this same way, once you get serious, you ought to know in six months if this person is someone you want to spend the rest of your life with. As I already said, don't be cruel. Don't waste five years of a woman's life and then leave her and get someone new. You ought to know in six months.

If you don't know in six months, then you must not know what you are doing, and you don't know what you are looking for.

4) Save Sex for Marriage -- It is much easier to break up with a woman if you have never had sex with

her. And sex can blind you from the truth. She may be severely lacking, but sex has a way of making up that deficit.

Sex helps when you are with the right person; sex does create that glue. But it can be dangerous if you are with the wrong woman. If you still want to see her every day, even though you are not having sex with her, then you know you really have something. If you see her every day and you still like her, and she is not driving you crazy, and you are not having sex with her, chances are, she is a winner.

5) Talk as Much as Possible – Since communication is the key, you need to know right away if you are going to be able to talk with one another. Once you have moved past the first four dates, and you are getting more serious about the person. You want to learn as much as you can, as well as be as honest as possible.

A relationship can be hard enough without a whole lot of surprises. I know that as men, we like a bit of mystery, and we can be concerned about sharing too much. And I understand that. I am not saying tell her your whole life story and every mistake you ever made in the first month. But what I am saying is that by the end of those six months, you ought to know enough about one another so that there are no surprises.

Chapter 5
Where's Waldo?

For women, the search is even more important, yet it is equally difficult. As you already know, being a woman in the 21st century is no easy task. You are expected to be tough and tender, serious and softhearted, a mother in the kitchen and a tiger in the bedroom. Men want it all, and if you are determined to have a man, you have to be ready to be it all.

That makes the search for you even more important. Much like the puzzle "Where's Waldo" there are plenty of distractions that can lead you away from the right man. A good man is truly hard to find, and time is of the essence.

Over the last few decades, women have been presented with more choices and more opportunities than ever. Women are running companies, serving as judges and doctors. Higher education has been something that they have been able to pursue. And although most women multi-task well, there is now a cultural effort to encourage them to focus on one thing at a time, which makes them choose one thing over the other. Women used to wonder if they could have it all, if they could they have a family and still have a career.

Now many women are thinking of career first with the hopes that they may be able to have a family in the future. And I am not saying that a woman's career pursuits are not admirable, nor are they misguided. What I am saying is that if you are going to have a man and a family, it may be something that you need to pursue. Just as you went after your education, your career, you are going to have to carve out time and attention to finding a man, or to really being found.

And time is of the essence. You don't have forever. At times, my counsel has even been to find the man and the family first. Think about it. You can always go back to school, but there is a limit to how long you can have kids. In this instance, ladies, time is not on your side.

Whenever I meet an attractive woman who is older than thirty, who has never been married, I always wonder about "the one that got away." Most women have one, a guy that was serious about them, but they were focused on other things, had other plans. They were so busy chasing other dreams that when the right guy came along, they assumed that they would eventually get another shot with another man.

But there is no guarantee that will happen. Ladies, you have to take every guy seriously. It is like Barry Bonds. I am not sure if you know who he is, but he was one of the greatest baseball players to ever play the game and one of the greatest homerun hitters who ever lived. What is even more remarkable is that not only has he hit more home runs than anyone else; he walked more than anyone else. A "walk" takes place when the pitcher throws four bad pitches, and you don't swing at them.

So what that means is that most of the pitches Barry Bonds saw were not very good pitches. So not only did he hit more home runs than anyone else, he hit them seeing fewer good pitches than anyone else.

Get my point? You have to see dating as your getting an opportunity to step to the plate. You are Barry Bonds. How many good pitches do you think you will get to swing at? You cannot afford to waste time and swings on bad pitches. When that right man shows up, you have to be ready to swing for the fences. Hit that home run, woman!

Of course, life and experience want to make you doubt and hesitate, wonder if you will ever meet the right man. And enough bad experiences can make you jaded, so tough that when you finally meet the right guy, you drive him away.

I totally understand the motivation behind women's liberation. Because women were being abused, neglected, treated as little more than property, they had to rise up and claim what was rightfully theirs. As men, we never should have put them in that place. But it is within our nature to abuse the power that we gain.

So I understand why a woman feels as if she has to watch out for herself. I understand why you may feel that you have to be hard, tough, and not let any man take advantage of you. You feel as though you can't just let some man take over your life, follow some man and his plan. And that sentiment is correct until you meet the right man for you.

If you meet him and you keep your walls up forever, then you may lose him. And then the pain caused you by the previous guys that hurt you will do more than just temporary damage. You want to limit the "ex-boyfriend" destruction as much as possible. Maybe he hurt you then, but that does not mean that you have to let that pain move forward with you. It is time to move forward. Believe that love is still possible.

The List

As a woman, your list is just as important as the men's list. And the reasoning is similar as well. If you are not looking for the right thing, you can fall for anything. Have a standard.

I grew up in a time when women had standards. A part of the reason a man did something or had a thing was because he was trying to impress a woman. When he met a woman for the first time, she would ask him certain questions, because she knew what she was looking for. She would ask, "What do you do? Do you have your own place? Is this your car? Where did you go to school?" Questions like that helped you to know that she had standards; there was something that she was looking for.

Now it is almost as if women are doing the chasing. You have to know who you are and what you are looking for so that there will not be an air of desperation that hangs around you like a cloud.

And that standard will help men to climb higher. If you don't make a list, if you don't have a standard, it affects society as a whole. Our culture is lessened when women become too easy or overly aggressive about love. Be ready to be found, but don't give the milk away for free. A part of the way you keep the value of a commodity high is to make sure that demand exceeds supply.

Now your list is going to differ from other women's, but there are some qualities that you must insist on in a good man. Allow me to help you see them clearly.

A Good Man...

1) Similar to you

Just as I said to the men, you don't want someone exactly like you. And that is impossible because men and women are very different, and as the French say, "Viva La Difference – Long Live the Differences." I am glad we are different, but we don't need to be so different that we cannot get along.

So just as I said to the men, if you are spiritual, he needs to be spiritual, if you love music, he needs to at least not hate music. If you love to stay home or just relax on vacation, then it would help if he has a similar vacation goal. Life is going to be tough if you end up with an adventure-seeking outdoorsman and you hate the woods.

2) Loving – Romantic

Men are looking for sex; women are looking for romance. I am not saying that women are not interested in sex, but romance is very important to you. Words are the way to your heart. You want a man who can at least communicate his feelings to you. You need someone who will treat you as the special, unique woman that you are.

If you need love, and you do, then it is foolish to involve yourself with a man who cannot express love to you. He needs to be good at expressing love in the way that you receive love. He needs to be open to learn how to love you, so that his love for you is never a question. And that love needs to be sacrificial. It is impossible to follow someone who does not love you at the expense of himself.

That love ought to make him caring and thoughtful. He needs to like you and be nice to you. His language with you ought to reflect the feelings he has for you. He should not speak to you as if you are his slave or his child. He ought to be respected by you, but that does not give him license to be disrespectful.

3) Tough – Dependable

A good man is like a Cyborg. I may have said that already, but it bears repeating. A Cyborg is metal robot wrapped in flesh. And that is what you are looking for, someone who keeps his word. You want a man who does not make a bunch of excuses, someone you can depend on.

Emotions are important, but you do not want a man so ruled by emotions that you cannot depend on him. You want someone you can trust—someone you know will be consistent, in spite of the circumstances.

There are so many men out there who will use any excuse to go back on the commitment that they made. You want to avoid those kinds of men—you want a promise maker and a promise keeper.

4) Employed with a Plan

Sometimes men can be intimidated by an educated, forward-thinking woman. And let's be honest, most of you are forward thinking. You want to know where this relationship is going; you want to know where we will be in five years, in ten years, in fifteen years. You want to know what the plan is.

And there are many of you who, if you do not see a plan, you will make one. Actually you probably have a plan already, so if you are going to change your life, change your plans, change your name, then this man needs to have a plan.

Because men need to be respected, you need to find a guy you respect, someone you think is smart— someone you believe knows what he is doing. And since responsibility and authority are connected, it is impossible to have one without the other. I am not saying that he needs to have all the responsibility, but he needs enough so that you can show him some respect and so that he will feel he is deserving of respect.

Some men walk around with a "respect" chip on their shoulders, and that is their own issue, a problem connected to their own failure. Unless he is lazy, an unemployed man will always be internally unhappy. You are not going to be able to make him happy, and eventually that will make you unhappy.

He does not have to make more money than you do. If you are highly educated and if you make a lot of money, then you are going to severely limit your options for a man if he has to make more money than you. He does not have to make more money than you, but he does need to bring enough to the table so that he can respect himself and so that you can give him the respect he needs.

5) Attractive

I trust that you are not bothered by the fact that I put Attractive fifth in this list. I just know women to be deeper. This is not to say that looks are not important to you; you do need to be attracted to the man. But women have that strength to be able to look past the exterior, to not judge the book by the cover.

But you do need to be attracted to him, for it is going to be much easier to be what he needs sexually if he is your type of guy in the first place. Also, the way he cares for himself is a sign as to how he will care for you. If you like clothes and shoes and fashion, then it probably would be a good idea to find a man that you consider "clean," someone who knows how to dress. He is going to want you to look good, because you will be a reflection of him, so he will not be as upset about your "clothes" bill.

Just realize that this is a double-edged sword, however. A man who gets his hair cut once a week is going to expect you to keep your hair done, and he is not going to be happy with a ponytail 90 percent of the time. It is amazing to me that the women who drool the most over the guys with the chiseled abs very rarely work out at all. If you meet a guy who is disciplined enough in his eating to have a six-pack, you had better be ready to stop eating desserts. And you need to take down all of your Facebook pictures of you with food.

6) Open

Woman, you know you are a mystery—you are a subject—which must be studied to be understood. When a man decides to be with you, he is going to the school of you. He has to be open, ready to learn new things. Each woman is like a combination lock. Once we master you, it is not a problem. But it takes time.

If he is going to be able to live with you, please you sexually, care for your children with you, understand what you mean, he is going to have to be open. If he is too closed off, ignorant, not ready to learn, overly stubborn, that is going to be a problem.

Women are always trying to bring some man to me for me to tell him something, a guy who has never listened to anyone. We know that most men are growing up without their fathers, but he needs to have someone he will listen to besides you. If he tells you, "I don't listen to anyone; I do what I think" then you need to run for the hills. He is going to be a tough man to live with.

He is going to listen to you about some things, but realize you are never going to be his mother. And that is a good thing because no man wants to sleep with his mother. Your influence is power, but you will need to know when and what battles to fight. If there is another voice that he will heed, be it God, his parents, a good friend, or a mentor, that is a good thing. You do not want to be the only voice of reason in his life. If you find him seeking and listening to advice, even if it is about you, you should respect that. That respect will help you in the future, and it is a sign that he is open.

You need to feel as if they have forgiven pains from the past, that they are open, and that they have let it go. No one wants to pay the back tax for some terrible previous relationship. If he speaks terribly about his mother, you want to sympathize, but eventually he needs to be healed and forgive. You don't want that anger pointed at you, and whether you want to admit it or not, there is a little bit of his mother in you.

7) Happy – Healthy

Most men are not overly happy, but that is something that we expect from women. We look for them to bring happiness into our lives. Even when we are satisfied, it is a temporary state for us. No matter how much money we make, we want more. Just because I went hunting last year and got a deer, does not mean I am not going back out to get another one. It is an exercise of restraint and discipline for us to have one woman. We always want more.

I trust that I did not scare you. My point is that an overly contented, too happy dude, may not have the drive you need to respect him. So you can't be surprised when he is not jumping up and down with joy and happiness all the time. But he should have a healthy perspective about life.

There should be some things that bring him joy. He ought to know how to rest, how to take a few days off and relax. And you should definitely feel as if he can find some joy in you. He ought to be happy to see you, and he should want to talk to you, spend time with you. You ought to feel that his happiness is a possibility.

Limits

If anyone needs to establish boundaries and limits, it is women. You all can be so loving and giving that if the rules are not established early, you will give everything away. You love that deeply.

But remember that your standard will call a man higher. Your limits are the same that I gave the men, but just with some different explanation:

1) One at a Time – Obviously you can't date four guys at once. And you need to stay away from your ex-boyfriends. They can clog your heart and actually block you from moving forward to new relationships.

At the same time, remember that just because a guy asks you to coffee does not mean that you should go buy your wedding dress and pick your colors. Stay open, but don't give your heart away so quickly.

And when it comes to love, you "Be the Too and not the You." What I mean by that is never say, "I love you" to a guy first. You say, "I love you *too*." Be the *too*, not the *you*.

2) Four Dates – Don't go out with a guy more than four times if it does not seem serious. Remember that you are not looking for more friends. Friends you have; you are looking for someone to spend the rest of your life with.

He ought to know, and you ought to know. You can tell right away if there is a connection. And remember, you can't possibly like or love someone enough for the both of you. He needs to like you, and you need to feel like he likes you. Don't settle for a guy you have to chase.

3) Six Months – Don't waste your time, and don't let a guy waste your time. For you, time is even more important, especially if you have not had children and you want some. Don't waste years of your life on some guy who is not serious. You ought to know where it is going in six months...

A real man who is looking for a commitment will always know in less than six months if he wants to be with you. He may stall a bit just so that he won't look crazy, or to really get his life in order, get his money right. But you will get a sense that he is serious about you and wants to be with you.

4) Save Sex for Marriage – This is so important for every woman to remember. Every time you let a man into your body, a piece of him gets into your soul. Women are more damaged by broken-off sexual relationships. It is easier to move on, and you are less humiliated, if you have not been intimate with the guy.

Maintain your integrity at all costs. If you are a virgin, stay that way. If you are not one, start from to today and be a virgin right now. There really is no rush to commit to you if I am already living with you and sleeping with you.

There was a time when that was the only way for a man to get consistent sex. When every woman had virtue, you couldn't get consistent sex unless you were married. And that was an incentive for the man to make the commitment. Stay true to yourself; it will protect your mind, body and soul.

5) Communicate – He ought to want to talk to you. You ladies have so much to say, and he ought to want to hear it. You have to know what to share with him, and what to share with your girlfriends. But still, consistent communication should be a standard that you hold onto.

You ought to be able to communicate your feelings, even when they are not great. Now don't get me wrong. A guy does not want to be burdened with all of your problems. He wants a happy woman. But at the same time, if there is something that is bothering you, you should be able to express it, and he should want to hear it.

There are a lot of men who avoid conflict at all costs. I am not saying that he should love confrontation and that you shouldn't be with a guy who needs a whole lot of confrontation from you anyway. You are not his mother. But he should not hate confrontation either. If you say, "We need to talk" he should want to hear you out so that problems are not allowed to linger and fester.

Finding Waldo is a challenge. But it is not impossible. If you believe in love, if you believe in yourself, then it is absolutely possible.

Chapter 6

Looking for Love

As previously stated, one of the greatest miracles of life is finding someone who is the match for you. Someone you love and like, someone who has strengths where you have weaknesses, someone you want to sleep with and talk and eat with. This truly is a rare thing. Humanity has used several methods to accomplish this monstrous task. For many years, love was not a part of it; marriages were arranged. Matchmakers were involved, and the parents handled it because people married for many reasons besides love.

As we have become more "enlightened" and I put that word in double quotation marks because I am not sure we are truly enlightened, but I digress. As we have reached our current perspective, love has become a key factor, an issue of choice. Whether or not that makes us more successful at marriage and family is another matter.

The point is, we now get to choose. We can go to places and try to meet people. We can even go online to dating websites, create a profile, and find someone. A friend can introduce us to someone, and that can often be a good way to meet someone, since a friend knows you and the other person. If they know you well enough, they can often make a good match.

There are so many ways this can happen, and I have met happily married couples that got together in all of the ways I mentioned. Since there are so many ways, it is even more important for us to lay down a few ground rules to help us stay true to we are and to keep our focus. So before we break down how to date successfully, let's just agree on some points to help us as we look for real, enduring love.

The Steps to Success:

1) Know who you are, and be yourself

Know your strengths, what you have to offer, but also be aware of your weaknesses. If you know that you have some things to work on, get busy. Don't wait until you have met someone to start working on your anger issues or your ability to be patient. Be the best you, so that you qualify for a great person.

Men – Gentlemen, it is going to be very difficult to explain yourself to someone if you are not sure who you are. How can a woman take you name if she does not know what that will mean? And the clearer you are about your destiny, the better you will be able to choose someone who can help you with that. If you are going to be a cop, then it does not make sense to be with someone who is full of fear, and worries all the time about your safety. A cop needs a cop's wife; a doctor needs a doctor's wife. I think you get the picture.

When you know who you are and what you want out of life, it provides focus to the process. And there is nothing worse as a guy than to just be motivated by the physical. There are so many different types of women out there, and it is absolutely possible to find what you are looking for; you just have to be smart about it.

It is as if you have been given $100,000. If I were to give you one hundred grand and tell you that you can buy any car you want, you will be wise to choose properly. If you said to me, "I am going to start a moving company, so I'm going to use this money to buy a truck with a hydraulic lift," I would say to you, "Wise move!"

If you then go to the dealership or an auction and come back with a Mercedes, and I ask you, "What happened to the truck?" and you said, "Well I went looking for a truck, but I just fell in love with this car," I will call you a fool. But that is often our perspective about love. I have even heard people say that, "You can't help who you fall in love with." That is pure nonsense. Keep your focus, know yourself, and know what you are looking for.

Women – It is even more important for you to know who you are and to be who you are. Men have the power of choice, but women have the power of change. You can change. Think about it; your body changes throughout the month. If you become pregnant, your body can adapt to hold and nourish another life. When the child is born, your body changes to produce milk. And as you age, your body changes to a point where your "mother" phase is at an end.

You have the power of change, and you can even change and adapt to situations. It is a part of your strength. Men know that, and we expect change. That is even a part of the foundation of women taking their husband's name. You are saying, "I accept that something has changed, I am not the same person I was; I have a new name."

Before you leap into change, you need to know who you are so that you can gauge the extent of the possibility of that change. If you are very extroverted and you meet a man who needs a quiet woman, you need to know your own limits. If you are extremely intelligent and are going after a high-powered, high-paying career, you need a man who is not intimidated by that. For him to ask you to stay at home when you have spent $250,000 on an education may be too big a change.

Men marry because they like what they have at that moment. And that is why men often feel as though they were duped or tricked. You need to be yourself, so that a man can like the real you. Don't make promises you have no intention of keeping. Stay true to yourself, and believe the right man will come for you. If you are determined to be a surgeon, then you need someone who is going to love you and be ready for quality time when it cannot be quantity time.

We can be very dishonest in our dating. Men and women, we can tell each other what we think the person wants to hear, even if it goes against who we really are. I am saying that is a recipe for disaster. Know yourself, like yourself; work on yourself.

2) Be Specific
We talked about this quite a bit in the chapter on lists, so I won't belabor the point. However, you need to be specific; know what you want in someone.

Specificity does not mean overly detailed pickiness. But you have to be careful not to be overly shallow and miss out on a good person because they do not have an overly specific detail like "light brown eyes." The list needs to be specific, but not rigid. You may have thought that you could only find what you were looking for in a certain country or a certain culture, but you could be surprised. We are the human race so someone from Asia or Australia may be the exact person for you.

Be specific, but stay open.

3) Look Good

You want to be honest, but still put your best foot forward. It is like when you are going on a job interview. You want the job, so you dress nice, get clean, and try to make a good impression. You are not trying to deceive; you are just trying to look your best. And what it took to get the job is what it will take to keep the job.

Now as important as a good job is, it is nothing in comparison to a life-long relationship. You don't have to stay at the job forever, but marriage you commit to. I know we want to just relax, but if you want to relax and look and smell and live any old way, then perhaps you should stay alone. When you bring another person into the picture, you are not just living for yourself; you are living for them as well.

That is one of the ironies of relationships in the 21st century. We want to be connected and still be individuals at the same time. When you love someone, you have to be aware of your appearance at all times.

Men – You want to look good, be clean, and have your plan together. Speak clearly; have some answers.

We all know women are going to ask questions, so try to anticipate those questions so that you have some good answers, so that you won't look foolish. Women want to know things like:

- Where do you work?
- Do you like your job?
- What do you like to do?
- Where do you see yourself in five years?
- Where is this relationship going?
- Do you like kids?
- What happened in your last relationship?

Be romantic, and stay romantic. Start the relationship off right by building within her some expectations for great things from you. Be a giver of gifts; be thoughtful. Set some good precedents early on. Good men can be creatures of habit. I started buying my wife flowers every Tuesday, about ten years ago. I just made it a part of my routine. We can be programmed to be thoughtful if we put our pride down long enough to accept some changes.

Women – Look your best. You know men are visual; don't complain about it; use that knowledge to your advantage. You don't have to dress like a prostitute, but don't be a Quaker either. Be consistent. Are you planning to wear make-up at your wedding? Why not start wearing a bit now? No one is saying you have to look like Halle Berry; just don't look like Marion Berry. You don't have to be Cindy Crawford; just don't be John Madden.

Be the best that you can be. Be virtuous. Work on the skills that men find attractive. Be nice, be friendly, smile. Men are motivated by fleshly desire. If you know men may have an expectation for a woman to know how to cook, you have a choice to make. You can either complain, call us Neanderthals, male chauvinistic pigs with antiquated expectations, or you can learn how to cook a few things.

Don't let pride get in the way of finding love. Remember that love is stronger than pride.

4) Be a Worker – Look for a Worker

Be determined not to be lazy. Know that building a relationship is going to be hard work. You are going to attract what you are.

Men – Even if you do not make six figures, a good woman can respect a hard-working man, someone who has a good job and works consistently. And a good woman wants to help; she wants to know how she can assist you with your life mission. She wants you to share your life with her so that she can actually make your life better.

Women – One of the worst things that can happen is to be a hard-working woman with a lazy man. You want a man that you can respect. And if he is a worker, that will help him to respect the work that you do. But you can't find a worker if you are not a worker.

I know that you are looking for your "king." But Kings marry Queens, and a Queen is the primary servant of the King. She is not treated as a servant, but she is still expected to serve.

A good relationship really is about giving. If you are not ready to give, you are not ready to love.

5) Watch

It is smart to watch for a while without words. If you can spend time with someone without a life-long commitment, it can help you to make a good choice. Some of the most happily married people I know started out as friends, then a romantic relationship grew out of that friendship. We can be so motivated by what we see, and then become so physically involved, that we did not take the time to really see what type of person we are getting involved with.

I know people who, because of the steps they have taken physically, begin to feel obligated to be in a relationship with a person so that they won't feel guilty about the quick sex. People have a tendency to get involved sexually and then trust that the rest will fall together. But that is not wisdom.

If you can, watch a person for a while, whether in church, at the job, or out in a group setting. See how that person interacts with other people; see how she is with other women and other men. What is her attitude? What does he say when someone talks about their children? If you have children, this would be a good time to watch and listen.

When we are putting our best foot forward in a dating situation, we can hide and cover. It is the natural thing to do. But in a more relaxed atmosphere where people are just friends, a person's true nature will come to the light. You want to try to see the real them before you commit your life forever.

I heard someone say, "You are the love of my life" and they had only known the person for less than six weeks. How could you possibly know that in six weeks? Remember that love is more than just a feeling, a physical attraction. Love is that decision you make once you really get to know the person, and see the things that may not be that great about them. For you to see those things, you may have to watch them a bit.

6) Check out the Family

My dad told me, "Son, before you commit to a woman, look at her mother. That is a glimpse into your future." Now I don't want you ladies to run right out and offend your mother by getting her a gym membership for Mother's Day. But your family is a factor in getting to know you.

Often, people wait until they are really serious about a person; then they want to meet parents. But I think it should be done sooner in the decision process. If you meet the family, there are several things that can happen.

Let's say you meet them and...

A) They are wonderful; you like them, and they like you. Then that is awesome, and you know you really have something with this person.

B) They are crazy

Your next question is, "Is she crazy like them? Is he crazy like they are?" The best way to gauge that is to bring up the *crazy* on the way back from meeting the crazy. If her response is, "What do you mean they are crazy?" If he gets defensive, "Hey that's my family, and I don't think there is anything wrong with them, you probably got crazy in your family too."

If that happens, then you probably want to get away from that person. They are probably as crazy as their family.

If their response is, "Yes, they are crazy, and that is why I almost did not want you to meet them" or "I know, that's why I almost never come over here," or "Yes, they are, and I have never really fit in. I am nothing like them." Those are all good responses; you probably can keep seeing them.

C) They are great, but you don't like how they live, or how they look. You don't like them.

Once again, you will have to mention this in as careful a way as possible. See what the response is. If the person you are dating agrees and assures you they are not going to end up like that, then you know you should continue to see them.

If they get defensive and try to emotionally manipulate you, then you need to be careful. I was talking to a young man who had and he met his girlfriend's mother, and he was worried because the mother was overweight. When he mentioned it to his girlfriend, she became very defensive, angry, and hurt. She began to defend why her mother was so heavy and was wondering if she should keep seeing him. She felt he was being shallow. He wanted to know what I thought he should do.

I told him that the needed to be careful. If she looks like her mother, has a similar build, and that is going to be a problem, then it is better to know it now. Remember that you have to be honest with yourself and know what you are going to be able to deal with. The anger and emotional manipulation would have been enough for me to reconsider the person. I know it was her mother, but we have to be able to love the people close to us, and still be honest about their shortcomings. I said to him, "If she agreed and said that she realizes her mother is overweight, but she is determined that is not going to happen to her, then that is a good thing, and you know you have a good woman. But the fact that she got defensive and angry, that is a sign of trouble."

D) They are great, but they don't like you

This is absolutely possible. If they don't like you, you have to take a hard look at yourself. Maybe you could have done a better job making a first impression. You may have to come back and apologize, see if they will give you a second chance. Marriage is tough to do with the person family aligned against you. If you can win them over, that would be wise.

That may not like you because they don't like anyone. Some people have parents like that. Some guys have mothers who do not think anyone is good enough for their son. Some parents don't like the idea of anyone trying to be with their daughter. And if that is the situation, then you will just have to be consistent. Know it is not you, and keep going. You will win them over eventually.

How people treat their family is also a window into the real them. If she is rude to her father or has never had a father, then you just learned something about her. How a man treats his mother and the way his mother treats him is important for you to know as a prospective wife. There is a lot that can be learned from these interactions. And it is even wiser if you can learn earlier than later.

7) Be Ready–Be a Doer

Understand that relationships have to keep moving. It is like treading water. A good swimmer can swim many laps for long periods of time, but it is very difficult to stay still, treading water in one place. In the same way, you can drown your relationship just by not moving forward.

What are you waiting for? Don't let fear keep you from making progress. Just because you have failed in the past does not mean that this may not be the person for you. Be ready to go. Be ready for change.

I know that you love your family and friends, but this relationship will have to become a priority. Some people are never able to move forward because they are too heavily tied to past relationships. Stop talking to your ex-; be ready for the new relationship that is waiting for your attention.

Remember your limits. You ought to know in seven to nine months if this person is the one for you. Look to the future, and start to plan now. It isn't just going to happen. You don't fall in love; you step into it with your eyes wide open.

Some Final Tips

Men

1) Let the Wiseman in you look. You know what your flesh wants; you know what your friends think. But there needs to be a decision made for the real you. Emotions and attraction are important, but let wisdom dictate.

2) Keep an eye on your list, but stay flexible.

3) Make a promise to yourself, know you, and don't go against yourself. Go into the situation in control of you. Value your seed; be determined not to share it with anyone but your wife. Marriage is about fidelity, so start getting ready by being celibate; be faithful to yourself. It is going to be tough to go from sleeping with any woman you want to just one woman for the rest of your life. But if you have been pure, the transition is not as difficult.

4) Be ready to give; know what you are bringing to the table. We ask a lot from women—be prepared to keep it balanced. You know you are not perfect; you just want the good to outweigh the bad.

5) Get busy. Get started today. What are you waiting for?

6) Don't be afraid to seek advice. There is a lot of information out there. Women should not be a total surprise to you. Know some things about all of them before you try to learn details about one of them.

7) Don't over commit too quickly. You get to choose; you have the responsibility. If this fails, it will be your fault. Take the job seriously. Try not to be overly rash.

Women

1) Be smart; keep your guard up until the right man comes along. I am not saying be closed, just don't be vulnerable. Nobody is saying that you should close the restaurant. Just don't let anyone in the kitchen until they buy the place. Understand? Vulnerability will have its place when you are married. For now, be wise.

2) Understand that a great woman is like Wal-Mart. At Wal-Mart you can get groceries and tires and something to wear. And that is what a guy is looking for, not one specific skill, but a well-rounded woman who has it together. I am not going to want to shop there if there is never any bread. Be complete.

3) Be beautiful – The visual is important. Men judge the cover. Stop complaining about it. Understand it. Deal with it.

4) Be a virgin, even if that starts today. Save the milk for the one who buys the cow. This analogy is not to call you a cow, but you understand my meaning.

5) Smile. Be happy. No one wants a miserable woman. No one is saying be easy, but don't be too difficult either. If a man smiles at you, smile back. Be nice.

6) Be ready for work. Get healthy in every way: physically and mentally. The saying is, "A man can work from sun to sun, but a woman's work is never done!" We expect you to be everything— "Bring home the bacon, and fry it up in a pan." God made you a woman because He knows you can handle the expectations.

7) Be ready for change. You are going to change, and you are probably going to be the one who changes first. But if you find the right man, he will change as well. Change is good; it is a sign of growth.

Chapter 7
Dating School

Once you have made your list, come to a firm conclusion on what you are looking for, next it is time to take the steps to secure it. Unfortunately, it is absolutely possible to find the right thing, and then mess up the situation by the way that you pursue it. Like in a court of law, just because you are right does not mean you are not "out of order." Getting things in the right order is as important as the thing itself.

Like the alphabet, when you learned it, you learned it in order, A B C D E F G, not M P T V S W K. You could say, "At least I know the letters." And that would be true, but not knowing the order can cripple your learning ability in the future. When it comes to dating, we tend to have this attitude. We don't care if we get the order of things wrong; we just want the stuff.

There are awesome benefits in a strong relationship. But for those benefits to be realized, the structure has to be put together properly. Just like building a house, you have to lay the foundation before you build the nice kitchen. If all you think about is your stomach and how wonderful the kitchen will be, you are going to end up with a house that will not last. The measurements have to be right; the plumbing and beams need to be level, and the concrete properly poured. Without the right structure and foundation, the kitchen will be the least of your problems.

But when it comes to dating, we have a tendency to be in a rush to "get to the kitchen." We want sex right away. I have even heard people say there is a three-date rule or a six-date rule: that rule being, three dates and then sex or six dates and then sex. Whether you think it is three dates or six or twelve, sex is not something you want to rush into without the proper foundation. The way that we date and get to know one another is the pouring of that foundation. It is the A B Cs of getting to know someone so that what we build will last.

Now I know what many of you are thinking. What about physical chemistry? How can I know if there is passion and chemistry with the person? How can I buy the car if I never get to drive it?

These are excellent questions, but I contend that it is possible to find passion without compromising your value system. No one is saying not to get in the car. I am not saying not to start it, maybe even drive it with the salesman in the car with you. I am just trying to keep you from taking the car home and putting your baby's car seat in it. Set some boundaries so that the ultimate goal can be achieved.

It comes back to our goal in dating. And at this point, you know what that goal is: marriage. If you are not interested in marriage then this book is not for you. We are talking about lasting relationships. So ask yourself, are you willing to sacrifice short-term sex for long-term marital bliss? Are you willing to be in a relationship that for a short period of time has boundaries when it comes to the physical, if it means long-term satisfying, long-lasting sexual happiness and true connection?

Let's do the math. According to several researchers, the average couple in America has sex less than four times a month. That is probably one of the reasons that divorce is at an all-time high and that there is so much marital unhappiness. But my point is that people started off so sexually involved that they were not able to build a lasting relationship. They built the kitchen and started eating, and then they tried to build the wall, and install the plumbing, and then the set-up the kids' rooms, etc. Is there any wonder that the house is falling apart?

I would rather spend the first year not having sex and then get married and spend fifty years having great consistent sex because we have built the relationship right. I would rather have that than having sex right away after three dates, eventually get married, and get to a place where we barely have sex at all.

I am not trying to make this whole dating chapter about sex. But as you continue to read, it is going to be very clear to you that I am trying to help you to date without sex. I am not doing that because I am a prude; I am doing that because I believe it is the best way to build a strong, long-lasting relationship.

The Rules

I know that some people hate rules. We want to be free to do whatever we want to do. But true freedom is not found in unbridled action. To really be free, you have to flow within some confines; otherwise, there can be no clear measure of victory. Just as in any sport, if there are not boundaries, then how can we establish the joy attached to winning? I want you to win in the game of love. For you to come out on top, you need to abide by a few rules:

I) The 99.9% Rules

There are a few things that you need to do almost 100% of the time to be successful. If you can follow the three simple guidelines, you will find yourself on the path to building a foundation for a real love relationship.

A) 99.9% of Dating Should Be in Public

This rule is the "trump card" when it comes to dating successfully. If you are going to avoid becoming overly physical and avoid rushing into sexual intimacy, public time is the key. It is absolutely possible to be alone in public. You can achieve all of the dating goals while still keeping this rule in place.

Pick her up in your car, and take her to a public place, a restaurant, the movies, a jazz club, a party at a friend's house, or an event at the church. Be together publicly, and when the date is over, take her home and say goodnight. Don't come in for a "cup of coffee" or to "talk for a minute." We all know where that will lead. Walk her to the door, and say goodnight.

B) 99.9% Sure of Marriage before Anything Physical

The most important thing to do with your mouth is talk to one another; learn to communicate. It does not take long to know if this person is the right person for you. I am not saying that you should be engaged after a few dates. But it does not take long to realize that this is someone you could spend the rest of your life with.

Kissing them definitely confirms that suspicion, but why kiss and "make out" with someone you can't see yourself having a future with? If after a few evenings the person is bothering you, and you don't seem to have anything in common, why would you get physically involved with them? You are just running the risk of creating a sexual attachment to someone who is not right for you.

I have seen it happen; people trying to turn a mostly sexual relationship into a long-lasting relationship. Is usually does not work. Until you have a strong sense that this is the person for you, keep your body under control.

C) 99.9% Knowledge of the Person

It is impossible to know everything about a person, but you can come pretty close. And you want to come close before you become overly involved. If you start to think that this is the one to whom you could say, "I do," then you really need to know that person. I am amazed at how many people are surprised after they are married to a person. You want to learn as much as you can before you take the final steps.

There are 7 things that I suggest you find out.

1) Personality – What is their personality? Are they an introvert? Are they outgoing, the "life of the party"? Does your personality fit with theirs? If they are loud and love to talk, do you like to listen to them? If they think they are funny, do you think they are funny? Believe me, your body parts fit together much easier than your personalities.

2) Perspective – Do you agree? Do you see the world in the same way? You will not be able to stay together if you do not agree. We will talk more about agreement in the next chapter on tests.

It is possible to challenge each other and change each other. A good relationship should help you to grow; you ought to be able to see more as a result of the love of this person. But at the same time, do not get ridiculous with it. If you believe in God and they do not, if you are a Republican and they are a Democrat, if you believe TV is a total waste of time and they love TV, your perspectives may be too opposite to build a lasting connection. You need to know how they see the world so that you can determine how to proceed. Don't be naïve; love can't conquer everything.

3) Potential – Where are they going? What plans have they made for the future? Will you be able to love who they are tomorrow? You might love this person in college, even in medical school, but will you be able to love them during their internship when you barely see them? Will you be able to stay with them during the residency when ninety percent of their time is spent at the hospital? It is not just about today; you have to factor in the future.

He may be a great athlete, but will he be a great father? She may be a great dancer, and look really hot in those jeans, but will she be a good mother? We rarely divorce the person we see right now. It is the tomorrow-person who we can't live with. And I believe you can see that tomorrow-person today. You can't just be with someone for who they are; you have to factor in who they are going to be.

4) Past – You should have a good grasp of where they have been. Who were they before you met them? How have they grown as a result of those experiences? Is he the same person he was in high school? If so, you need to run for the hills. Some people are extremely proud of the fact that they have not changed. Certainly there are some good qualities that you want people to maintain, but we all still need to grow and change.

And if they have not examined their own past, they may be doomed to repeat it. If they are, say, divorced, you need to know that you are nothing like their ex. Why would you put them in that situation again?

Experiences drive expectations. You need to know what has happened so that you can be prepared for what they will expect. Sometimes we can be careful about what we disclose, and I understand that caution. But at some point, you have to trust the person enough to be honest with them.

5) Parents – How were they raised? We are a reflection of our parents. Certainly, we can grow beyond them and become more than they ever were, more than they ever could be. But there is a little bit of your father on the inside of you. You can't help it; it is DNA, as well as the way they raised you.

We have talked about this already in a previous chapter, so I won't repeat myself. But just remember, their parents are a factor in who they are and who they will be. If their parents always fought, then that may be their expectation for relationship. You need to know what they saw growing up, if for nothing else, for them to guarantee to you that they will not be that way.

6) Patterns – You need to see them in their routine. This is a part of the challenge of a long-distance relationship. You need to see how your life will fit around their normal life schedule, and vice versa: how their life will fit around your life schedule. What are the activities that normally dominate their time? If they work a lot, you need to see that pattern now and know how you fit.

Most of us are creatures of habit; we are pretty consistent. You need to like the routine that you build. Boredom can be a real hindrance to long-lasting love. You need to understand the routine so that you can avoid falling into a rut that will cause you to stray. At the same time, there needs to be a comfort with the routine. There is nothing worse than one person being happy with the norm, while the other person is miserable. I have seen that happen; people who thought the marriage was happy, but found out that while they were happy, their partner was not.

7) People – Who do they like to hang with? Who are their friends? If you don't like his friends, you probably don't like him either. He is just not showing you all of himself. So if you find yourself saying, "I can't stand any of his friends; I am glad he is not like them!" I am sorry to tell you this, but he is like his friends. They wouldn't be friends if they were not the same.

"Birds of a feather flock together." That is a true statement. You need to meet the friends. If you like her friends, and her friends like you, then that is a good foundation. As much as you are going to be friends, she is still going to need her girl friends. If she has to make a choice between them and you, that can be a long-term problem. You may feel good about the fact that she chose them over you, but you are going to find yourself as the only person she can talk to. And believe me, man; you do not want that to be the case.

II) The Commandments of Dating

Let me give you some final overall guidelines to dating properly. I grew up aware of the ten commandments, so I thought I would phrase them in that way, perhaps to help you to remember them.

1) Be You – Make a commitment to yourself first. Be determined to hold to your standard: check your list; refuse to compromise. You can't find your match if you can't love and accept who you are right now.
2) Create Relational Intimacy – Go out to coffee, lunch, dinner; talk on the phone; Skype. Do whatever you have to do to create a relational connection. Talk more than you touch.
3) Do Not Rush – Don't over commit too soon. Someone suggested to me on Facebook that if people wait to have sex, they might rush into marriage just to have sex. I absolutely disagree. Sex can certainly be an incentive to find the right person, but there have been many more relationships that have been rushed because people have not waited to have sex.

You want to take your time, get to know the person. Just because someone asks you to coffee does not mean that you should start looking at reception halls. Remember that love is a decision. You are not trying to fall in; you are trying to step in.

4) Keep an Eye on the Clock – You are not rushing; yet at the same time, this should not take forever. See the relationship in phases.
Dating Phase: 2-3 months at the most
Committed/Pre-Engagement/Exclusive Phase: 3-12 months.
Engagement Phase: 6-9 months

What I mean is that within a year, you ought to be moving to marriage. If you date for three months, then spend from month four until month fourteen in an exclusive relationship; that is sensible. You could be engaged six moths after meeting someone, but that may be rushing it a bit. I would want to at least know someone for a year before I commit my life to him or her. Maybe if the person was someone I already knew, we were friends, came from the same town, or went to high school together, those scenarios may allow for a quicker decision.

And I really don't think you should be engaged any longer than it takes to plan a wedding. Once you have made that commitment to one another, what are you waiting for?

If you can see someone every day for ninety days, without sex, and they don't drive you crazy, you really know you have something. Don't rush, but don't drag your feet either. You don't have forever. Within eighteen months, you ought to be married.

5) Honor your Father and Mother – Meet the parents; let them meet your parents. Maybe even have the parents meet each other. Respect the wisdom and advice you get from the people who love you, especially if they have some wisdom.

If your mother hates the man you are dating, that needs to be considered. Maybe she sees something that you do not see.

6) Public Privacy – Be alone in public. Stay out of each other's homes, apartments, and bedrooms. Go out, and then say good night.

Group dating can help. Spend time with other couples. Find friends who are trying to date the right way. Support and encourage one another.

7) Do Not Double Time – Don't date more than one person at a time. Marriage is about monogamy. How can you focus and make the right choice if you are juggling three people at once. Give the relationship the respect of your undivided attention.

8) Do Not Lie – Be transparent. Be honest. Let them see the real you, not your agent.

9) Stay Open – Be ready for change. Just because you know who you are right now does not mean that you will not grow. Don't say what you will never do. You don't know what you will do for someone who is your match. True love is stronger than pride.

10) Test – Don't be afraid to test the relationship. If you can't pass any tests, then you can't graduate to the next level.

Chapter 8
This is a Test

When I was in school, especially middle school and high school, I hated tests. Once I got to college, I still wasn't in love with tests, but I understood the function of the test. Because I knew I was paying for my education, I had a better attitude about the test. I realized that the test was a tool to help me to learn. The test was a way for the university to prove to me that they had taught me the material I was paying them to teach me. A lot of times, we feel judged by tests, and in a sense, the test does judge you; the teacher is judging you; the university is judging you. But if you understand that actually you are the one who is in control since you are the one seeking education, it can help you to have a better attitude about a test.

And I said all of that to make this point. If we are afraid of tests, and if we are determined to avoid them at all costs, then we will never benefit from the test. When something is "tested" it is proven sound. Before they sold you that car you are driving, it went through some tests. The brakes were "tested" to make sure they would work consistently. Before the plane takes off, the pilots put it through a few "tests." They want to make sure that all of the systems are functioning properly;

they don't want something to happen when they are in the air.

In that same way, a serious relationship should be "tested." You don't want to be in the air, ten years in with kids on board, and find our your flaps are not working. Understand? Many relationships crash because before they took off the pilots did not do the proper "pre-flight" systems tests. As the pilots, you and this person you love have to do your "pre-flight" system tests. Before you take off into marriage, let's do the tests. Do you want to graduate from an amazing relationship, to a healthy marriage? Then take the final exams, earn the degree.

The Tests

I) The Agreement Test

Probably the biggest question to ask is, "Do we agree?" All of these tests are important, but the Agreement Test is probably the most important of them all, and that is why I am listing it first.

Connecting your life to another is extremely challenging. You are already different. Men and women are clearly different. You come from different families. You may come from different areas. If you are from different cultures, that is another great difference. If you have different personalities, different levels of education, or have had different experiences in relationships in the past, it can be a hindrance to unity. You want to start with as much agreement as possible.

Communication is a challenge, and we will talk about that in a moment, in "The Communication Test."

But before we do that, let me just mention that it is going to be much easier to communicate if you start off in agreement. It does not matter how mature you are or how much you love one another; if you spend too much time communicating about things that you do not agree about, it can turn ugly quickly. The key is to agree.

Agree about what? Excellent question. Here is a list.

My suggestion to couples who are dating and getting to know one another is that you go into the relationship with a contemplative smirk on your face. Do not be naïve; a great relationship is not easy to find. It takes chemistry; it takes patience; it takes communication. Don't assume everything is great; don't walk into it with a big assuming, sappy smile on your face. Walk into this thing with a SMIRK:

S – Sex
M – Money
I – Intangibles
R – Religion
K – Kids

Sex

You need to have an open, honest conversation about sex. You need to talk about what you have experienced. You need to talk about what you expect. If one of you believes that sex should happen five times a week, and the other person thinks it should happen five times a month, that is a big gap to bridge. You want to be in agreement.

What will your sex life include; what is available; what is on the menu? If you expect oral sex, massages, different positions, etc., you need to be up front about your expectations. If your partner is looking for something that you are uncomfortable about providing, be honest. Find out if it is a deal breaker. But you also want to be careful about declaring what you would never do. You don't know. Love has a way of making the unthinkable very thinkable; the undoable becomes extremely doable.

When you are talking about sex, you are also talking about attraction. If this guy likes long hair, if she likes you with a beard, are you ready to adapt to her needs? If you are not ready to be what this person needs you to be, you may need to reconsider whether this is the person for you. Maybe you are telling your girlfriends, "Yeah, girl, he wants me to work out, but I don't know; that's a lot of work." If you are saying something like that, you need to question whether he is the person for you. Maybe you need to work out, and he is providing the motivation that you need to help you do what you need to do.

But you need to be ready to handle this person's opinion of you. You need to want to be with them physically. You need to like how they look now and tomorrow. I know that when we talk about physical attraction, we mostly think of this as a "guy thing." We expect women to be deeper. Guys are the ones that we see as "shallow," needing the woman to look a certain way.

But I think physical attraction is equally important for the woman. As a woman, if you marry a normal, fully heterosexual male, you are going to have to be prepared to have sex, and lots of it, especially if you want to be a good wife and want for him to be happy. You may have to have sex when you are tired, not quite in the mood. It is going to be much easier to be a "Yes" girl if you are seriously attracted to the man in the first place. Maybe it is so easy to say no to the guy because he doesn't make your heart skip a beat.

Guys like to believe that they are irresistible to their woman. You don't want to reject a guy too much; it can make him not like you. The man's penis and his self-esteem are often connected. If you reject his penis, ultimately you are rejecting him. And if you reject him too often, he will eventually replace you with someone who will not reject him. And that is a part of why pornography is so popular. It is not just because men are so visual and sexual. It is also because those women don't have "problems"; they didn't have a "stressful day at work." Those women just say "Yes," they say "Please, more." I know it is a fantasy; it is unrealistic. Men know that. It is unfair to ask you to compete with that. I am not asking you to compete with it, I am saying be aware of it. You don't have to be a "Porn Star"; you just can't be a "NO Star."

Gentlemen, when we are talking about sex, we are talking about romance. Are you ready to write poetry? Are you ready to give flowers? Are you ready to take her on vacation, listen to her talk, sympathize with her? Are you ready to create and maintain relational intimacy?

A wife said to me once, "The only time he touches me is when he wants to have sex with me."That husband is a fool. That is like going to the doctor only when you feel sick. That is like only looking under the hood of the car only when it starts to smoke. Anything worth having has to be maintained. I don't ever want my wife to think that or say that. I have to hug her, hold her hand and touch her face.

And that is the added challenge of pornography. It is unrealistic. Those women are not real. No pizza delivery guy walks up to the door and gets a "blow job" as a tip. That does not happen. No quality woman is quick, easy, and free. Anything worth having has a price. I enjoy sex with my wife; we have a great sexual relationship. But I am no fool. I realize that a great sexual relationship is a result of a great relationship. You can't have one without the other.

Money

You need to agree about money. If one person wants to spend and the other person wants to save, that is a big divide to bridge. You need to agree about how you will spend your money, how you will save your money, and how you will invest your money. Financial stress can put serious strain on a marriage. You need to be as wise as possible about your money decisions, and you need to agree.

I touched on this briefly, but when we are talking about money, we are also talking about career decisions. What if she has an opportunity in North Dakota? Are you prepared to move to North Dakota? What if he is trying to be a surgeon? What if he wants to be a career soldier, what if she wants to fight in the war in Iraq? Are you prepared for that possibility?

I was talking with a couple who was dating. I asked her what she wanted to do with her life. She told me she wanted to be an actress. I said, "Well if you are going to be an actress, you will have to live in California or New York." She replied, "Exactly!" So I turned to the guy, and I asked him, "Are you ready to live in New York? Do you want to live in California?" He said, "I never want to live in either of those places!"

So I said, "Well, then, you two probably don't need to be together. Someone is going to end up resenting the other person. Either she is going to give up her dream of being an actress for you, or you are going to be dragged to live places you do not want to be." They were not in agreement.

I know we just believe that "Love will conquer all," but that is not true. Love can be destroyed by a lack of agreement.

Intangibles

The little things do mean a lot, especially when other problems are prevalent. Ever know a couple that split up over something that seems trivial? I have. But what I realize is that often, the trivial thing was the "straw that broke the camel's back.

It never ceases to amaze me how people will be in a relationship with a person who does the very things that set their teeth on edge. If you are a "neat freak" then it probably doesn't make sense to marry a slob. If the sound of gum being chewed drives you crazy, then maybe you shouldn't marry someone who lives for gum. If you are a "homebody" then you don't want to end up with someone who wants to go out every night. Yes you will change, yes they will adapt to you. But they shouldn't have to change their whole personality.

Religion

Wars are fought over God. You don't want your marriage to be a holy war. If one person believes in God, and the other person does not, that is a problem. If one person is a Christian, and the other person is a Muslim, that is going to be a real problem. If he wants to go to the Baptist church, and you want to go to your grandmother's Catholic church, that can be a potential problem. You need to discuss and agree on what you believe.

Kids

If he wants five children, and you do not want any, that is potential for a real problem. We usually discuss how many children we want. The bigger issue is usually how we raise children. You certainly need to agree about that. We have a tendency to parent the way that we have been parented. So if you believe in spanking and she believes in "time-out," that can be a potential problem. You need to agree.

If you have children from a previous relationship, there needs to be agreement. If you do not trust him to discipline your son, then maybe you do not trust him.

The opposite-sex parent has a tendency to be softer. Mothers are softer on sons and harder on daughters. She feels that her little girl is going to be a reflection of her. In the same way, guys are harder on boys and softer on their daughters. He may be hard on your son just because he is a boy. The kids are a big deal and there needs to be agreement.

Wow, I did not expect that Agreement Test to be so lengthy, but then again, it is the most important test. Let's look at a few more so that you can be prepared.

II) The Communication Test

How well do you communicate? That is the next question. If you can agree and communicate, then nothing can stop you. You and your mate may find yourself at the body of water called *Disagreement*. Communication and understanding are the bridge to get you across that body of water.

Let's be honest. You are not going to agree about everything. But you can still adapt and change, even if you do not agree. If you can only change because you agree, then you are immature. Mature people can adapt simply because they understand.

But for there to be understanding, there has to be effective communication. Can you communicate? Here are some signs that you have a serious communication problem.

A) You fight and argue a lot, more than once a month. Once a month may not sound like a lot, but it is. Many of us grew up with either no couple to emulate or a couple who constantly argued and fought. That may make great comedy or drama on a TV show, but it is not conducive to real life love and marriage.

Fighting is a sign that you either do not agree on some major issues or you cannot communicate with each other without getting angry. Remember what I said in the Agreement Test. Even the most mature couple can "get into it" if they spend too much time discussing something they do not agree about. At the time of this writing, my wife and I have been married for twenty-one years. We get along great. It is September 2012, and we have probably had one major argument all year. We have been doing this a while, and we are very compatible, although we are very different. So don't be too hard on yourselves. My point is that if we spend too much time discussing something we do not agree about, even though we love each other and we are both mature, there is still a time limit. It can turn ugly if it goes on for too long.

If you cannot compromise, find the middle ground. However, that can be a real problem. I may not agree with everything my wife says, and she certainly does not agree with me all the time. But thankfully, we can communicate well enough to understand one another. And we adapt because we can communicate and understand.

B) That leads us to another sign, though: an inability to compromise. Love is stronger that pride. If you love one another enough and if it is meant to be, then pettiness is not a factor. I can compromise; it does not always have to be my way. We talked, and I understood, so I moved.

C) Great sex, bad talk. Sometimes you will see someone in a movie or on TV who says, "We need to stop talking and just respond." That can be a dangerous way to live real life. The physical should not be the best part of your relationship. As a guy, you might think you want sex with silence, but in the long run that is not the case. There are plenty of men who stop being intimate with their wives because of the way the wife makes them feel, but it is more than just physical.

D) Certain things we just can't talk about. If you find yourself saying, "I guess we just can't talk about that," that is a dangerous sign. You should be able to talk about anything. Nothing should be off limits. Even if you are not super comfortable about talking about something, it should never be taboo.

Most people who have a marriage problem have either an agreement problem or a communication problem. If you can start your relationship off with great agreement and great communication, you have won half the battle.

III) The Logic Test

Does this make sense? I know some great things can happen that are illogical, but that is the exception. If you are saying, "I know this is crazy, but I just want to try" think again. If he lives in Japan, and you have known him only three weeks, but you just "feel like something is telling you to go for it," chances are you do not know what you are talking about.

You need to do the math.

"Well, she is old enough to be my mother, and I don't even like tall women, but we just have something special." That statement is dangerous. "I have never met him; we have just written each other emails, but he asked me to marry him, and I just felt right about it." Woman, think again.

Most things that sound crazy are crazy.

IV) The Love Test

This may seem obvious, but you need to make sure you really love them. You need to be unable to imagine life without them. You need to love everything about them, not just a few things.

When you love someone, you love…

A) Their Name – Something happens when you hear their name called. You want your name attached to their name. You want her to be your wife, to have your name. She is connected to you; she is a good reflection of who you are. You do not hear her name and feel shame.

You are not afraid to take his name. You want to change; you are ready to be something that you have not been before. His name is just that valuable to you. You feel pride in him. When you become a couple and people mesh your names together: Steve and Cheri, Andy and Lashawn, Bill and Linda, you feel good about it.

B) Their Words – When they talk, you want to listen. You like the things they say; you like the things that they like to talk about. The fact that they "always want to talk about that" does not bother you. You understand who they are and where they are coming from. She is a teacher; she likes to talk about her students. He is a mechanic; he likes to talk about the car problem he fixed today. She is a lawyer; she wants to talk about the law. He is a political analyst; he does not get on your nerves talking about the Clintons.

I saw a Klondike Bar commercial in which a guy spends five seconds listening to his wife, just to get a Klondike bar. While he is listening, he is sweating, breathing heavy, like he is running a marathon. When the five seconds are over, he jumps in the air and screams, "Yes, I did it!" Listening to your wife talk should not be the "thing you will do to get a Klondike bar." You should like to hear them talk.

Understand? If you don't like what they have to say, you are not going to want to stay with them. If you can't wait for them to just "Shut *up!*" then maybe you don't really love them.

C) To Make Them Happy – Marriage is not about being selfish. If I am trying to make her happy and she is trying to make me happy, then we will both be happy. But if I am just trying to make myself happy and she is just thinking about her own happiness, we will turn on one another.

When you love someone, their smile actually brings joy to you. It is tough to function in a world where she is miserable. If she is unhappy and you don't care, if he is miserable and you say, "Well, whatever"—you probably don't love them. Maybe you just love yourself.

D) To Spend Time with Them – It is not a chore to be around them. You actually like to be around them; you want to know where they are. When will they be back? Will they be gone long? You are comfortable in their presence; you feel as if you can relax and really be yourself. If you are glad when they leave and sad when they get back, you may be settling, because you probably do not love them.

E) Their People – When you meet their family, their friends, you like them. It is tough to love someone when you do not love who they love. If she loves her mother and wants to still spend time with her, that is fine as long as you don't hate her mother. If you never want to be around his friends, that may be a problem. If you say, "I don't know how you can be around them," that can be a potential problem.

They may know people you do not know and love some people that you tolerate. But it can be tough if you feel disgust for someone they adore.

F) You are Willing to Change – Actually you barely notice the change. You adapt and don't really think about it. You wake up years later and realize they have changed you. Of course, those changes need to be positive changes. But if they are overly stubborn, absolutely refuse to change, then they may not really love you.

They want you to do all the changing because they love themselves, not you.

G) You Will Sacrifice – Love is not love if it does not cost something. Real love always has some pain attached to it. The sacrifice does not even seem like sacrifice. The love you have for the person makes it all worth it.

Conclusion—Find Love

Let me say a few final words. I trust these previous thoughts have helped you.

Luther Vandross had a song entitled, "Wait for Love." Don't settle; love is absolutely possible. Don't let the depiction of relationships in the media dissuade you from finding that person for you. Love is possible.

But when you find it, cherish it. This is the biggest decision you will ever make. You don't want to make it too many times. For many of us, by the time we get married, we have "been in love" several times; we have not saved ourselves sexually; we have loved and lost. Why not take this moment to leap frog into a new belief system. You have done it your way. Has it worked?

I may have suggested some things that you have heard before, or some of this may be crazy and brand new. But what do you have to lose?

We are failing as a generation, especially in America. We are failing at the most important thing ever created, something we all need, love. And our children are being impacted by our failure; our health is being affected by our failure; our money is being affected by our failure.

But is not too late for us. We can turn it all around.

I wish you all the best that love has to bring. Real Love is worth the wait; Real Love is worth the sacrifice; Real Love is worth the cost. And you are worth it. You deserve it. Don't settle for anything but the best: Real Love.

e|LIVE

listen|imagine|view|experience

AUDIO BOOK DOWNLOAD INCLUDED WITH THIS BOOK!

In your hands you hold a complete digital entertainment package. In addition to the paper version, you receive a free download of the audio version of this book. Simply use the code listed below when visiting our website. Once downloaded to your computer, you can listen to the book through your computer's speakers, burn it to an audio CD or save the file to your portable music device (such as Apple's popular iPod) and listen on the go!

How to get your free audio book digital download:

1. Visit www.tatepublishing.com and click on the e|LIVE logo on the home page.
2. Enter the following coupon code:
   64b4-a778-8b69-c46a-0bbf-99cc-3858-1eaa
3. Download the audio book from your e|LIVE digital locker and begin enjoying your new digital entertainment package today!

CPSIA information can be obtained
at www.ICGtesting.com
Printed in the USA
FFOW03n1252161016

9 781618 628022